VEGETARIAN FEAST

VEGETARIAN FEAST

150 DELICIOUS RECIPES SHOWN
STEP BY STEP IN MORE THAN
200 STUNNING PHOTOGRAPHS

VALERIE FERGUSON

southwater

This edition is published by Southwater, an imprint of Anness Publishing Limited,
Hermes House, 88–89 Blackfriars Road, London SE1 8HA
tel. 020 7401 2077; fax 020 7633 9499;
www.southwaterbooks.com; www.annesspublishing.com

If you like the images in this book and would like to investigate using them for publishing, promotions or advertising,
please visit our website www.practicalpictures.com for more information.

UK agent: The Manning Partnership Ltd; tel. 01225 478444; fax 01225 478440; sales@manning-partnership.co.uk
UK distributor: Grantham Book Services Ltd; tel. 01476 541080; fax 01476 541061; orders@gbs.tbs-ltd.co.uk
North American agent/distributor: National Book Network; tel. 301 459 3366; fax 301 429 5746; www.nbnbooks.com
Australian agent/distributor: Pan Macmillan Australia; tel. 1300 135 113; fax 1300 135 103; customer.service@macmillan.com.au
New Zealand agent/distributor: David Bateman Ltd; tel. (09) 415 7664; fax (09) 415 8892

Publisher: Joanna Lorenz
Editor: Valerie Ferguson
Recipes contributed by: Catherine Atkinson, Alex Barker, Michelle Berriedale-Johnson, Angela Boggiano, Kathy Brown, Carla Capalbo, Kit Chan, Jacqueline Clark, Carole Clements, Trish Davies, Roz Denny, Patrizia Diemling, Matthew Drennan, Sarah Edmonds, Rafi Fernandez, Christine France, Silvano Franco, Shirley Gill, Nicola Graimes, Rosamund Grant, Carole Handslip, Rebekah Hassan, Deh-Ta Hsuing, Shehzad Husain, Christine Ingram, Judy Jackson, Manisha Kanani, Sheila Kimberley, Sara Lewis, Patricia Lousada, Lesley Mackley, Sue Maggs, Kathy Man, Sally Mansfield, Norma Miller, Sallie Morris, Annie Nichols, Maggie Pannell, Katherine Richmond, Jennie Shapter, Anne Sheasby, Liz Trigg, Hilaire Walden, Laura Washburn, Steven Wheeler, Elizabeth Wolf-Cohen, Jeni Wright
Photography: William Adams-Lingwood, Karl Adamson, Edward Allwright, Steve Baxter, Nicki Dowey, James Duncan, John Freeman, Ian Garlick, Michelle Garrett, John Heseltine, Amanda Heywood, Ferguson Hill, Janine Hosegood, David Jordan, Dave King, Don Last, Patrick McLeavey, Michael Michaels, Steve Moss, Thomas Odulate, Simon Smith, Sam Stowell, Polly Wreford
Designer: Carole Perks
Typesetter: Diane Pullen
Editorial Reader: Linda Doeser
Production Controller: Claire Rae

ETHICAL TRADING POLICY
Because of our ongoing ecological investment programme, you, as our customer, can have the pleasure and
reassurance of knowing that a tree is being cultivated on your behalf to naturally replace the materials used to
make the book you are holding. For further information about this scheme, go to www.annesspublishing.com/trees

© Anness Publishing Limited 2002, 2008

A CIP catalogue record for this book is available from the British Library.

NOTES
Bracketed terms are intended for American readers.

For all recipes, quantities are given in both metric and imperial measures and, where appropriate, in standard cups and spoons.
Follow one set of measures, but not a mixture, because they are not interchangeable.

Standard spoon and cup measures are level. 1 tsp = 5ml, 1 tbsp = 15ml, 1 cup = 250ml/8fl oz.

Australian standard tablespoons are 20ml. Australian readers should use 3 tsp in place of 1 tbsp for measuring small quantities.
American pints are 16fl oz/2 cups. American readers should use 20fl oz/2.5 cups in place of 1 pint when measuring liquids.

Electric oven temperatures in this book are for conventional ovens. When using a fan oven, the temperature will probably need to be
reduced by about 10–20°C/20–40°F. Since ovens vary, you should check with your manufacturer's instruction book for guidance.

Medium (US large) eggs are used unless otherwise stated.

Main front cover image shows Fragrant Lentil & Spinach Salad – for recipe, see page 87

Contents

Introduction

Never before has vegetarian food been so exciting, imaginative and appetizing. As we have discovered the varied cuisines of the world and the health-giving benefits of a vegetarian diet, the meat-free recipes of each country have been added to the adventurous cook's

repertoire. In response to growing culinary interest, the ingredients often required for ethnic dishes are now available in supermarkets and specialist food stores, making it easy to re-create the fresh flavours and stunning colours of the Mediterranean, the spicy tastes of Mexico, India and South-east Asia and the piquancy of the Caribbean islands.

In this book you will find inspiring recipes using a breathtaking variety of ingredients including fresh vegetables, fruit, herbs, nuts, seeds, pulses, grains, tofu, dairy produce, pasta and noodles that make the most of seasonal goodness. There are warm and filling soups, pies and casseroles for the cold winter months and light, refreshing salads, dips, and pasta dishes for perfect *al fresco* summer eating.

The book is divided into five chapters. Soups, Dips & Snacks offers a tempting selection of recipes, from delicate Cream of Courgette Soup and rich Blue Cheese Dip to spicy Guacamole and Mexican Tortilla Parcels. In Quick & Easy you will find recipes that can be rustled up in just a

few minutes using fresh and store-cupboard (pantry) ingredients – ideal for a quick after-work meal or to satisfy a hungry and demanding family. There are classic omelettes, tasty frittatas and stir-fries as well as pasta and speedy rice creations. Midweek Meals take a little longer but are worth the effort. The recipes can be used for family meals or for informal entertaining. Enjoy the comfort of a Vegetable Crumble, an

unusual savoury Tomato Bread & Butter Pudding, moreish Cheese & Leek Sausages with Spicy Tomato Sauce and Butternut Squash & Sage Pizza. When you want to impress your guests with your culinary skills turn to Special Occasion Dishes for inspiration. Here you will find a mouthwatering collection of soufflés, crêpes, risottos, stuffed vegetables and melt-in-the-mouth tarts for every kind of party or

celebration and to suit all tastes. Many of the dishes can be prepared in advance, leaving you plenty of time to spend enjoying the company of your guests rather than in the kitchen.

The final chapter, Side Dishes, Salads & Bread, is bursting with great ideas for the mainstay of vegetarian cooking. It features flavoursome options from all over the world including the Spanish way of preparing spinach, a delicious courgette (zucchini) dish from Italy and crisp Eastern European potato pancakes as well as aromatic Indian and Indonesian rice dishes. You can choose from salads that range from the fresh and light to more substantial grain and bean combinations including Fattoush, Feta & Mint Potato Salad and Couscous Salad. Bread is the ideal accompaniment to many vegetarian dishes, which often have a delicious sauce that is too good to waste. The breads in this section focus on classics from around the world.

In addition, there is a useful opening section describing a wide variety of popular and less familiar vegetarian ingredients, and techniques for preparing food as well as basic recipes that you will use again and again. Whether you are a committed vegetarian or someone who enjoys innovative cooking using interesting ingredients, this inspiring book will help you to create food for pleasure and health.

The cardinal rule when shopping for vegetarian ingredients is to choose the freshest possible produce, buying little and often. For dried goods, find a supplier with a healthy turnover, so stocks don't have time to get stale. Keep a constant lookout for new and exciting products. Vegetarian food is a growth market, and the range of available foods is constantly increasing. Once the preserve of the health food store, vegetarian ingredients are now stocked in every supermarket, and the demand for organic produce, and products made from organic ingredients, is huge.

Vegetables & Fruit

Buy the bulk of your produce from local growers, if possible, balancing home-grown vegetables and fruit with exotic imports. Some supermarkets support local growers, including organic ones, so look for labels that state the provenance of the produce. Several organic farms offer box schemes, where you opt to buy a box of vegetables and/or fruit every week. What goes into the box depends on what is being harvested at the time, and because everything is picked to order, it is beautifully fresh. This is a great way of buying greens, such as spinach or Swiss chard. Farmer's markets are excellent sources of fruit and vegetables, as are allotment shops, where growers sell their surplus. If you live in the country, keep an eye open for roadside stalls. Gardeners often grow vegetables not generally available in the stores, such as the more unusual types of squash, and sell them at very reasonable prices. Pick-your-own vegetable farms aren't as common as those offering pick-your-own fruit, but corn on the cob is sometimes sold that way. Don't forget essential aromatics such as fresh garlic and root ginger.

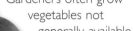

tomatoes

Swiss chard

winter squash

garlic

apples

aubergines (eggplant)

Herbs & Spices

The most satisfying way to obtain herbs is from your own garden. You don't need acres of space as even a window-box or a few pots on the patio will yield a generous harvest. Obvious candidates are mint and parsley, preferably the flat leaf variety, but you should also aim to grow thyme, basil, sage and oregano or marjoram. If you possibly can, add coriander (cilantro), chives, chervil, tarragon, rosemary and bay, all of which feature in this book. Alternatively, buy herbs from the supermarket, but use them as soon as possible after purchase. Dried herbs lose their potency quite quickly, so buy small amounts at a time, keep them in a cool, dry place (out of direct sunlight) and replace them as soon as they start to go stale.

For the best flavour, buy whole spices and seeds, and grind them as needed in a spice mill or coffee grinder kept for the purpose. Dry-frying spices before grinding intensifies their flavour. Essential spices include cardamom pods, cumin and coriander seeds, cinnamon sticks, nutmeg, dried chillies and chilli powder, cayenne, paprika, Chinese five-spice powder, garam masala, saffron, turmeric and curry powder.

basil

flat leaf parsley

cinnamon

chives and bay leaves

coriander seeds and leaves

Clockwise from top: celery seeds, chilli powder, chilli flakes and cayenne

Grains, Pasta & Pulses

The dried versions of these easy-to-use ingredients are store-cupboard (pantry) staples. Rice is invaluable to the vegetarian cook, both as a base for vegetable stews and sautés and for stuffed vegetables. In addition to regular white and brown long grain rice, try basmati, which has a wonderful fragrance and flavour. Rinse it well before use and, if there is time, soak it in the water used for the final rinse. For risotto you will need a short grain rice such as arborio, carnaroli or Vialone Nano. Bulgur wheat has already been partially prepared, so needs only a brief soaking before use. It is the basis for tabbouleh, and also tastes good in pilaffs and baked dishes. Another great grain that needs very little preparation is couscous, which is made from coarse semolina.

rice

dried pasta

lentils

Dried pasta comes in an astonishing array of shapes. Some of the more unusual types are introduced in recipes in this book, but you can always substitute whatever you have in the cupboard. Dried egg noodles are essential for many Asian dishes.

Fresh pasta is becoming widely available. Find a reliable source and buy it as needed, or make your own, using our basic recipe. Pulses, such as dried beans, split peas and lentils, keep well and play a vital role in vegetarian cooking. Most pulses need to be soaked overnight, so remember to take the time into account when you are planning your menu.

dried beans

From the Refrigerator & Freezer

Dairy products provide lacto-vegetarians (those who eat dairy produce) with valuable protein, calcium and vitamins B_{12}, A and D, but can be high in fat. Like eggs, they should be eaten in moderation. Look out for vegetarian versions of your favourite cheeses (produced with vegetable rennet). Yogurt, crème fraîche and fromage frais are also very useful, as is tofu, a protein-rich food made from soya beans. Various forms are available, from soft silken tofu to a firm type which can be cubed and sautéed. Tempeh is similar to tofu, but has a nuttier taste. Keep filo pastry, unsweetened shortcrust and puff pastry in the freezer, but allow plenty of time for slow thawing. Nuts will also store well in the freezer.

parmesan cheese

tofu

sour cream and crème fraîche

From the Pantry

If your store cupboard is well stocked, spur-of-the-moment meals will never be a problem. In addition to pasta, pulses and grains, dry goods should include different types of flour, easy-blend (rapid-rise) dried yeast, polenta and oatmeal, and you'll also want a small supply of nuts. Don't buy these in bulk, as nuts become rancid if stored for too long. Dried mushrooms are useful, as are sun-dried tomatoes and (bell) peppers, but you may prefer to buy the ones that come packed in oil in jars. Also in jars, look for pesto (both green and red), tahini,

mixed nuts

canned beans

peanut butter, capers and olives. Useful sauces include passata (bottled strained tomatoes), creamed horseradish, soy sauce in various strengths, black bean sauce and the vegetarian versions of oyster sauce and Worcestershire sauce. You'll need a variety of vinegars, including red and white wine, balsamic and rice vinegar; and oils, especially olive, sunflower, sesame, groundnut (peanut) and walnut oil. For low-fat cooking, a light oil spray is useful.

Cans take up quite a lot of space, but it is well worth keeping a stock of favourites, such as tomatoes, kidney beans, borlotti beans and chickpeas, plus corn kernels, artichoke hearts and bamboo shoots. Canned coconut milk comes in handy for curries and some soups.

wine vinegar

Techniques

Even the simplest tasks in the kitchen can take longer than necessary if you don't know a few useful techniques and short cuts. Below are some step-by-step instructions for preparing a variety of ingredients that will save time and help to improve the presentation of the final dishes. No special equipment is required for most of them, just a sharp knife.

Chopping Onions

I Cut a peeled onion in half lengthways and place one half, cut-side down, on a board. Slice it vertically several times.

2 Make two horizontal cuts in from the stalk end towards the root, but not through it. Holding the onion by the root end, cut it crossways to form even diced pieces.

Cutting Vegetable Batons

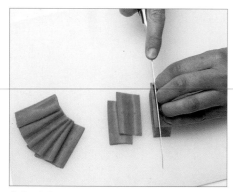

I Peel firm vegetables and cut in 5cm/2in lengths. Cut these into 3mm/⅛in slices.

2 Stack the slices and cut them neatly lengthways into thin strips.

Peeling & Chopping Tomatoes

I Cut a cross in the blossom end of each tomato. Put them in a heatproof bowl and pour over boiling water.

2 Leave for 30 seconds, until the skins wrinkle and start to peel back from the crosses. Drain, peel off the skin and chop the flesh neatly.

Chopping Herbs

I Remove any thick stalks and discard. Pile the herbs on a board and chop them finely, first in one direction, then the other, using a sharp knife or a mezzaluna (half-moon herb chopper), which you use in a see-saw motion.

Blanching Vegetables

I Bring a pan of water to the boil. Using a wire basket, if possible, lower the vegetables into the water and bring it back to the boil.

2 Cook for 1–2 minutes, then drain the vegetables and cool them quickly under cold running water or by dipping them in a bowl of iced water. Drain well.

Roasting & Peeling (Bell) Peppers

I Leave the peppers whole or cut them in half and scrape out the cores and seeds. Place them on a grill (broiler) rack under medium heat, turning them occasionally, until the skins are evenly blistered and charred but not too burnt, as this will make the flesh taste bitter.

2 Seal the peppers in a plastic bag or place them in a bowl and cover them with several sheets of kitchen paper. When the steam has softened them, peel off the skins. Remove the bitter seeds if necessary, working over a bowl to catch any juices. The juices can be used in a salad dressing.

Crushing Garlic

1 Break off a clove of garlic and smash it firmly with the flat side of the blade of a cook's knife. Pick off all the papery skin.

2 Chop the clove coarsely, sprinkle over a little table salt, then use the flat side of the knife blade to work the salt into the garlic until it is reduced to a fine paste.

Preparing Chillies

1 Wearing rubber (latex) gloves if possible, halve the chilli lengthways. Leave the seeds inside or scrape them out and discard them.

2 Slice or chop the chilli finely. Wash the knife, board and your hands (if not gloved) in hot soapy water, as chillies contain a substance that burns sensitive skin. Never rub your eyes or touch your lips after handling chillies.

Preparing Fresh Root Ginger

1 Using a vegetable peeler or a small knife, peel the skin off a piece of fresh root ginger. Cut the ginger in thin slices.

2 Place each slice on a board. Cut it into thin strips and use, or turn the strips around and chop them finely. Ginger can also be grated, in which case it need not be peeled.

Preparing Lemon Grass

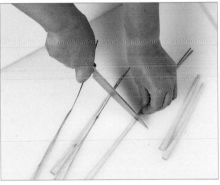

1 Discard any tough outer layers from the lemon grass stem, then cut off the end and trim the top, leaving a piece 10cm/4in long.

2 Split this in half lengthways, then chop very finely. If the bulb is particularly fresh, it can be thinly sliced. Whole stems can be used for flavouring and removed before serving.

Crushing Spices

1 Dry-fry whole spices in a heavy frying pan, then put them in a mortar and grind them with a pestle to make a smooth powder.

2 Alternatively, grind them in a spice mill or a coffee grinder kept specifically for the purpose. Use a pastry brush to remove all the ground spice from the inside of the grinder.

Preparing Pulses

1 Rinse well, pick out any small stones, then put the pulses in a bowl with plenty of cold water. Soak for 4–8 hours.

2 Drain the pulses, rinse them under cold water and drain them again. Tip them into a pan. Add plenty of cold water but no salt. Bring to the boil, boil hard for 10 minutes, then simmer until tender. Drain and season.

Cook's Tip
Lentils do not need to be soaked before cooking. Red lentils become very soft when cooked and are ideal for purées. Green or brown lentils are firmer and retain more texture. The finest flavoured are Puy lentils.

Basic Recipes

The recipes in this book are largely complete in themselves, but there are a few basics that crop up again and again, such as vegetable stock, tomato sauce, flavoured oils, and doughs for pizzas and pasta. You can, of course, substitute bought ingredients, such as sauces, ready-made pasta and pizza bases, but do make your own if you have time as they taste great.

Pizza Dough
Makes 1 x 25–30cm/10–12in round pizza base

175g/6oz/1½ cups strong white bread flour
1.5ml/¼ tsp salt
5ml/1 tsp easy-blend (rapid-rise) dried yeast
120–150ml/4–5fl oz/½–⅔ cup
　　lukewarm water

1 Sift the flour and salt into a bowl and stir in the yeast. Add the water and mix to a soft dough. Knead on a floured surface for 10 minutes, until smooth and elastic. Return to the clean bowl, cover with lightly oiled clear film (plastic wrap) and leave in a warm place for 1 hour, or until the dough has doubled.

2 Knock back (punch down) the dough, knead it for 2 minutes, then roll it out to a 25–30cm/ 10–12in round. Place on a greased baking sheet and knock up the edges. Top and bake as suggested.

Cook's Tip
Mix and knead the dough in a food processor, if you like, but transfer it to a bowl for rising.

Pasta Dough
Serves 6

300g/11oz/2¾ cups Italian *Tipo 00* flour or
　　strong white bread flour
5ml/1 tsp salt
3 eggs, beaten

1 Put the flour and salt in a food processor fitted with the metal blade. Pour in one egg, cover and pulse to mix on maximum speed. Add the remaining eggs through the feeder tube and mix briefly to form a dough.

2 Knead the dough for 5 minutes if you are shaping it in a pasta machine and for 10 minutes if shaping by hand.It should be very smooth and elastic. Wrap it in clear film (plastic wrap) and leave to rest for 15–20 minutes before rolling it and cutting it into shapes.

Making Pasta Dough by Hand

1 Mound the flour on a work surface, make a well in the centre and add the eggs and salt. Mix with your hands or a fork, gradually incorporating the surrounding flour until a rough dough forms. Knead as in the main recipe.

Tomato Sauce
Makes about 350ml/12fl oz/1½ cups

15ml/1 tbsp olive oil
1 onion, finely chopped
1 garlic clove, crushed
400g/14oz can chopped tomatoes
15ml/1 tbsp tomato purée (paste)
15ml/1 tbsp chopped fresh mixed herbs
　　(parsley, thyme, oregano, basil)
pinch of granulated sugar
salt and ground black pepper

1 Heat the oil in a pan and cook the onion and garlic gently until softened. Stir in the tomatoes, tomato purée, herbs and sugar, with salt and pepper to taste.

2 Simmer, uncovered, for 15–20 minutes, stirring occasionally, until the mixture has reduced and is thick. Use at once or cool, cover and store in the refrigerator.

Cook's Tip
Use this tomato sauce on pizzas or pasta. It is excellent in lasagne, and tastes good with vegetables. Spoon it over cooked cauliflower, top with grated cheese and grill (broil) until bubbly.

Vegetable Stock
Makes about 2.4 litres/4 pints
2 large onions, coarsely chopped
2 leeks, sliced
3 garlic cloves, crushed
3 carrots, coarsely chopped
4 celery sticks, sliced
a large strip of pared lemon rind
12 fresh parsley stalks
a few fresh thyme leaves
2 bay leaves
2.4 litres/4 pints water

1 Put the onions, leeks, crushed garlic cloves, carrots and celery slices in a large pan or flameproof casserole. Add the strip of pared lemon rind, with the parsley, thyme and bay leaves. Pour in the water and bring to the boil. Skim off the foam that rises to the surface.

2 Lower the heat and simmer for 30 minutes. Strain the stock, season to taste and leave to cool. Cover and keep in the refrigerator for up to 5 days, or freeze for up to 1 month.

Cook's Tip
To save freezer space, boil vegetable stock down to concentrate it to about half the original quantity and then freeze in ice cube trays. When thawing add an equal amount of water.

French Dressing
Makes about 120ml/4fl oz/ ½ cup
90ml/6 tbsp olive oil or a mixture of olive and sunflower oils
15ml/1 tbsp white wine vinegar
5ml/1 tsp French mustard
pinch of granulated sugar
salt and ground black pepper

1 Place the oil and vinegar in a screw-top jar. Add the mustard and sugar.

2 Close the lid tightly and shake well. Season to taste.

Mayonnaise
Makes about 350ml/12fl oz/1 ½ cups
2 egg yolks
15ml/1 tbsp Dijon mustard
30ml/2 tbsp lemon juice or white wine vinegar
300ml/ ½ pint/1 ¼ cups oil (vegetable, corn or light olive)
salt and ground black pepper

1 Put the egg yolks, mustard, half the lemon juice or vinegar and a pinch of salt in a blender or food processor and process for 10 seconds to mix. With the motor running, add the oil through the feeder tube, drop by drop at first and then in a steady stream, processing constantly until the mayonnaise is thick and creamy. Taste and sharpen with the remaining juice or vinegar, if you like, and season to taste.

Chilli Oil
Makes about 150ml/ ¼ pint/ ⅔ cup
150ml/ ¼ pint/ ⅔ cup olive oil
10ml/2 tsp tomato purée (paste)
15ml/1 tbsp dried red chilli flakes

1 Heat the oil in a pan. When it is very hot, but not smoking, stir in the tomato purée and chilli flakes. Leave to cool.

2 Pour into a small jar or bottle. Cover well and store in the refrigerator for up to 2 months (the longer you keep it the hotter it gets).

Garlic Oil
Makes about 120ml/4fl oz/ ½ cup
3–4 garlic cloves
120ml/4fl oz/ ½ cup olive oil

1 Peel the garlic cloves and put them into a small jar or bottle. Pour in the oil, cover securely and store in the refrigerator for up to 1 month.

SOUPS, DIPS & SNACKS

Many of the world's favourite soups, from French Onion Soup to Chinese Hot-&-sour Soup, are vegetarian, perhaps because vegetables and pulses seem such natural and trouble-free ingredients to use. Undoubtedly, it also has something to do with the fact that they smell so appetizing, look so attractive and taste so delicious. They are also extremely easy and often very quick to make. The secret of success is to use a good vegetable stock as the basis. Best of all, make your own and then you can be sure of exactly what ingredients have gone into it and, just as importantly, what has been left out, such as preservatives, colourings and an unhealthy quantity of salt. While home-made soup is always a welcome treat, especially on cold winter evenings, sometimes the occasion calls for a cold appetizer. Whether you are planning a dinner party or simply want to make family supper a little more special, you will find the perfect recipe in this chapter. A fabulous collection of dips, from smooth and mellow to hot and spicy, can be made in next to no time and will turn any occasion into a party. Finally, this chapter includes a range of more substantial hot snacks with an international theme. From Middle Eastern Falafel to Potato Skins with Cajun Dip, these dishes are perfect for parties, ideal for entertaining unexpected guests and hit the spot when you are feeling peckish

French Onion Soup

This classic French soup is popular the world over. It is always served with a slightly chewy topping of melted Gruyère cheese.

Serves 4
50g/2oz/ ¼ cup butter
2 onions, about 250g/9oz total weight, sliced
10ml/2 tsp plain (all-purpose) flour
1 litre/1¾ pints/4 cups Vegetable Stock
60ml/4 tbsp dry white wine or 30ml/2 tbsp dry sherry
4 slices crusty white bread
150g/5oz/1¼ cups grated Gruyère or Emmenthal cheese
salt and ground black pepper

1 Melt the butter in a large, heavy pan. Add the sliced onions and cook over a moderately low heat, stirring occasionally, for about 12 minutes, or until lightly browned. Stir in the flour and continue to cook, stirring constantly, for 10–12 minutes, until the flour turns a sandy colour.

2 Pour in the stock and wine or sherry, then bring to the boil, stirring constantly. Season to taste with salt and pepper, cover and simmer for 15 minutes.

3 Spread out the slices of bread in a grill (broiler) pan and toast them lightly. Divide the grated cheese among them. Return to the grill and heat until the cheese is bubbling. Place the cheese toasts in four warmed, heatproof bowls.

4 Using a slotted spoon, scoop out the onions from the soup and divide them equally among the heated bowls. Pour over the soup and serve immediately.

> **Cook's Tips**
> • *To give the soup a good colour, make sure the onions are lightly browned before you add the stock.*
> • *Grated mature (sharp) Cheddar cheese can be substituted for Gruyère or Emmenthal, but neither the flavour nor the texture will be strictly authentic.*

Cream of Courgette Soup

The joys of this soup are its delicate colour, creamy texture and subtle taste.

Serves 4–6
30ml/2 tbsp olive oil
15g/ ½oz/1 tbsp butter
1 onion, coarsely chopped
900g/2lb courgettes (zucchini), trimmed and sliced
5ml/1 tsp dried oregano
about 600ml/1 pint/2½ cups Vegetable Stock
115g/4oz Dolcelatte cheese, rind removed, diced
300ml/ ½ pint/1¼ cups single (light) cream
salt and ground black pepper
fresh oregano and extra dolcelatte, to garnish

1 Heat the oil and butter in a large pan until foaming. Add the onion and cook gently, stirring frequently, for about 5 minutes, until softened but not brown.

2 Add the sliced courgettes and dried oregano and season with salt and pepper to taste. Cook over a medium heat, stirring frequently, for 10 minutes.

3 Pour in the stock and bring to the boil, stirring constantly. Lower the heat and partially cover the pan. Simmer gently, stirring occasionally, for about 30 minutes. Stir in the diced Dolcelatte until melted.

4 Pour the mixture into a blender or food processor. Process until smooth, then press through a sieve into a clean pan.

5 Add two-thirds of the cream. Stir over a low heat until hot, but not boiling. Check the consistency and add more stock if the soup is too thick. Taste for seasoning, then pour into heated bowls. Swirl in the remaining cream. Garnish with fresh oregano and extra cheese and serve immediately.

> **Cook's Tip**
> *There are vegetarian versions of a wide variety of cheeses. Look for them in large supermarkets or health food stores.*

Butternut Squash Soup

The rich golden colour, creamy texture and mild curry flavour combine to make this soup a winter winner with all the family.

Serves 6

1 butternut squash
1 cooking apple
25g/1oz/2 tbsp butter
1 onion, finely chopped
5–10ml/1–2 tsp curry powder
900ml/1½ pints/3¾ cups
   Vegetable Stock
5ml/1 tsp chopped fresh sage
150ml/¼ pint/⅔ cup
   apple juice
salt and ground black pepper
curry powder and finely shredded
   lime rind, to garnish
Curried Horseradish Cream
   (optional), to serve

1 Peel the squash, cut it in half and remove the seeds. Chop the flesh. Peel, core and chop the apple.

2 Heat the butter in a large, heavy pan. Add the onion and cook, stirring occasionally, for 5 minutes, until soft and translucent. Stir in the curry powder. Cook, stirring constantly, for 2 minutes.

3 Pour in the stock, then add the squash, apple and sage. Bring to the boil, lower the heat, cover and simmer for 20 minutes, until the squash and apple are tender.

4 Process the soup in a blender or food processor to a smooth purée. Return to the clean pan and add the apple juice. Season with salt and pepper to taste. Reheat gently, without allowing the soup to boil.

5 Serve the soup in heated bowls, topping each portion with a dusting of curry powder. Garnish with a few lime shreds. Add a spoonful of Curried Horseradish Cream, if you like.

> **Cook's Tip**
> Butternut squash looks rather like an oversize, elongated yellow pear. It is descriptively named, as the deep golden-yellow flesh has a buttery consistency and a nutty taste. However, other varieties of winter squash could also be used in this soup.

Curried Horseradish Cream

This is particularly good as a topping for the Butternut Squash Soup, but can be used with other vegetable soups as well. It is also excellent as a dipping sauce for crudités – use double or treble the quantity.

Serves 6 as a topping
60ml/4 tbsp double (heavy) cream
10ml/2 tsp creamed horseradish
2.5ml/½ tsp curry powder

1 Whip the cream in a bowl until stiff, then stir in the creamed horseradish and curry powder.
2 Cover and chill in the refrigerator for up to 3 days.

Spiced Lentil Soup

A subtle blend of spices takes this warming soup to new heights. Serve it with warm crusty bread for a satisfying lunch.

Serves 6

2 onions, finely chopped
2 garlic cloves, crushed
4 tomatoes, coarsely chopped
2.5ml/½ tsp ground turmeric
5ml/1 tsp ground cumin
6 cardamom pods
½ cinnamon stick
225g/8oz/1 cup red lentils
900ml/1½ pints/3¾ cups water
400g/14oz can coconut milk
15ml/1 tbsp fresh lime juice
salt and ground black pepper
cumin seeds, to garnish

1 Put the onions, garlic, tomatoes, turmeric, cumin, cardamom pods, cinnamon and lentils into a pan. Pour in the water. Bring to the boil, lower the heat, cover and simmer gently for about 20 minutes, or until the lentils are soft.

2 Remove the cardamoms and cinnamon stick. Process the mixture in a blender or food processor to a smooth purée. Press the soup through a sieve, then return it to the clean pan.

3 Reserve a little of the coconut milk for the garnish and add the remainder to the pan, together with the lime juice. Stir well. Season to taste with salt and pepper. Reheat the soup gently without boiling. Ladle into heated bowls, swirl in the reserved coconut milk, garnish with the cumin seeds and serve.

> **Cook's Tips**
> • For maximum flavour, use sun-ripened vine tomatoes, rather than those ripened under glass. Alternatively, stir in a little tomato purée (paste) or use canned tomatoes.
> • When whole cardamom pods are used for flavouring – usually in soups and casseroles – they are removed before serving or processing to a purée. The small black seeds – usually used for flavouring desserts – may be eaten.
> • The cooking time for lentils may vary, depending on how long they have been stored.

Corn & Potato Chowder

This creamy yet chunky soup is rich with the sweet taste of corn. Serve it hot, topped with grated cheese.

Serves 4
30ml/2 tbsp sunflower oil
25g/1oz/2 tbsp butter
1 onion, chopped
1 garlic clove, crushed
1 medium baking potato, chopped
2 celery sticks, sliced
1 small green (bell) pepper, halved, seeded and sliced
600ml/1 pint/2½ cups Vegetable Stock or water
300ml/½ pint/1¼ cups milk
200g/7oz can flageolet or cannellini beans
300g/11oz can corn kernels
good pinch of dried sage
salt and ground black pepper
grated Cheddar cheese, to serve
fresh sage leaves, to garnish

1 Heat the oil and butter in a large heavy pan. Add the onion, garlic, potato, celery and green pepper and cook over a low heat, stirring occasionally, for about 10 minutes, until the onion is softened and golden.

2 Pour in the stock or water, season with salt and pepper to taste and bring to the boil. Lower the heat, cover and simmer gently for about 15 minutes, until the vegetables are tender.

3 Add the milk, beans and corn – including the can liquids. Stir in the sage. Simmer, uncovered, for 5 minutes. Serve, sprinkled with the grated cheese, garnished with sage leaves.

> **Cook's Tip**
> Although the word "chowder" is most closely associated with a soup made from clams, this recipe contains the two traditional ingredients – vegetables and milk – so it is quite authentic.

> **Variation**
> If you are unable to locate canned flageolet or cannellini beans, use frozen peas instead.

Ribollita

Ribollita is an Italian soup, rather like minestrone, but with beans instead of pasta. It is traditionally served ladled over bread and a rich green vegetable.

Serves 6–8
45ml/3 tbsp olive oil
2 onions, chopped
2 carrots, sliced
4 garlic cloves, crushed
2 celery sticks, thinly sliced
1 fennel bulb, chopped
2 large courgettes (zucchini), thinly sliced
400g/14oz can chopped tomatoes
30ml/2 tbsp home-made or ready-made pesto
900ml/1½ pints/3¾ cups Vegetable Stock
400g/14oz can haricot (navy) or borlotti beans, drained
salt and ground black pepper

To finish
15ml/1 tbsp extra virgin olive oil, plus extra for drizzling
450g/1lb fresh young spinach
6–8 slices white bread
ground black pepper

1 Heat the oil in a large pan. Add the onions, carrots, garlic, celery and fennel and cook gently for 10 minutes. Add the courgettes and cook for 2 minutes more.

2 Stir in the chopped tomatoes, pesto, stock and beans and bring to the boil. Lower the heat, cover and simmer gently for 25–30 minutes, until the vegetables are completely tender. Season with salt and pepper to taste.

3 To serve, heat the oil in a heavy frying pan and cook the spinach for 2 minutes, or until wilted. Put a slice of bread in each heated soup bowl, spoon the spinach on top, then ladle the soup over the spinach. Offer extra olive oil at the table, so that guests can drizzle it on to the soup. Freshly ground black pepper can be sprinkled on top.

> **Variation**
> Use other dark greens, such as Swiss chard or cabbage, instead of the spinach; shred and cook until tender.

Borlotti Bean & Pasta Soup

A complete meal in a bowl, this is based on a classic Italian soup. Traditionally, the person who finds the bay leaf is honoured with a kiss from the cook.

Serves 4

75ml/5 tbsp olive oil
1 onion, chopped
1 celery stick, chopped
2 carrots, chopped
1 bay leaf

1.2 litres/2 pints/5 cups
    Vegetable Stock
400g/14oz can
    chopped tomatoes
175g/6oz/1½ cups dried
    pasta shapes
400g/14oz can borlotti
    beans, drained
250g/9oz fresh young spinach
salt and ground black pepper
50g/2oz/⅔ cup freshly grated
    Parmesan cheese, to serve

1 Heat the olive oil in a large, heavy pan and add the chopped onion, celery and carrots. Cook over a medium heat, stirring occasionally, for 5 minutes, or until the vegetables soften and the onion is translucent.

2 Add the bay leaf, stock and tomatoes and bring to the boil. Lower the heat and simmer for about 10 minutes, until the vegetables are just tender.

3 Bring the soup back to the boil, add the pasta shapes and borlotti beans and simmer for 8 minutes, until the pasta is *al dente*. Stir the soup frequently to prevent the pasta from sticking to the base of the pan.

4 Season to taste with salt and pepper, add the spinach and cook for 2 minutes more. Serve in heated bowls, sprinkled with the grated Parmesan.

Variations
• *Add a glass of white wine with the stock, if you like.*
• *Substitute two shallots for the onion and ½ small fennel bulb for the celery.*

Garlic, Chickpea & Spinach Soup

Tahini, sesame seed paste, is the secret ingredient that gives this thick, creamy soup such a superb taste.

Serves 4

30ml/2 tbsp olive oil
4 garlic cloves, crushed
1 onion, coarsely chopped
10ml/2 tsp ground cumin
10ml/2 tsp ground coriander
1.2 litres/2 pints/5 cups
    Vegetable Stock

350g/12oz potatoes, chopped
425g/15oz can chickpeas,
    drained and rinsed
15ml/1 tbsp cornflour
    (cornstarch)
150ml/¼ pint/⅔ cup
    double (heavy) cream
30ml/2 tbsp light tahini (sesame
    seed paste)
200g/7oz fresh young
    spinach, shredded
salt and ground black pepper
cayenne pepper, to serve

1 Heat the olive oil in a large, heavy pan. Add the garlic and onion and cook over a medium heat, stirring occasionally, for 5 minutes, or until the onion has softened and is golden brown.

2 Stir in the cumin and coriander and cook for 1 minute more, then pour in the stock. Add the potatoes. Bring to the boil, lower the heat and simmer for 10 minutes.

3 Add the drained chickpeas and simmer for 5 minutes more, or until the potatoes are just tender.

4 Mix the cornflour, cream and tahini in a bowl. Stir in plenty of seasoning. Stir the mixture into the soup and add the spinach. Bring to the boil, stirring constantly, then simmer for 2 minutes. Ladle the soup into heated bowls, sprinkle with a little cayenne pepper and serve immediately.

Variation
Ful medames would make a delicious alternative to chickpeas, but you would probably have to use dried beans. Soak them overnight and then simmer for 3–4 hours before using.

Hot-&-sour Soup

This spicy, warming soup is the perfect introduction to a simple Chinese meal. Cloud ears are a type of Chinese fungi.

Serves 4
10g/ ¼oz dried cloud ears
8 fresh shiitake mushrooms
75g/3oz tofu
50g/2oz/ ½ cup sliced, drained, canned bamboo shoots
900ml/1 ½ pints/3¾ cups Vegetable Stock
15ml/1 tbsp caster (superfine) sugar
45ml/3 tbsp rice vinegar
15ml/1 tbsp light soy sauce
1.5ml/ ¼ tsp chilli oil
½ tsp salt
pinch of ground white pepper
15ml/1 tbsp cornflour (cornstarch)
15ml/1 tbsp cold water
1 egg white
5ml/1 tsp sesame oil
2 spring onions (scallions), sliced into fine rings

1 Soak the cloud ears in hot water to cover for 30 minutes or until soft. Drain, trim off and discard the hard base from each and chop the cloud ears coarsely.

2 Remove and discard the stalks from the shiitake mushrooms. Cut the caps into thin strips. Cut the tofu into 1cm/ ½in cubes and shred the bamboo shoots finely.

3 Place the stock, shiitake mushrooms, tofu, bamboo shoots and cloud ears in a large, heavy pan. Bring the stock to the boil, lower the heat and simmer for about 5 minutes.

4 Stir in the sugar, vinegar, soy sauce, chilli oil, salt and pepper. Mix the cornflour to a paste with the water. Add the mixture to the soup and stir constantly until it thickens slightly.

5 Lightly beat the egg white, then pour it slowly into the soup in a steady stream, stirring constantly. Cook, stirring constantly, until the egg white changes colour.

6 Add the sesame oil just before serving. Ladle the soup into heated bowls and top each portion with spring onion rings, then serve immediately.

North African Spiced Soup

Warm spices, such as cinnamon and ginger, give this thick vegetable and chickpea soup an unforgettable flavour.

Serves 6
1 large onion, chopped
1.2 litres/2 pints/5 cups Vegetable Stock
5ml/1 tsp ground cinnamon
5ml/1 tsp ground turmeric
15ml/1 tbsp grated fresh root ginger
pinch of cayenne pepper
2 carrots, diced
2 celery sticks, diced
400g/14oz can chopped tomatoes
450g/1lb floury potatoes, diced
5 saffron threads
400g/14oz can chickpeas, drained and rinsed
30ml/2 tbsp chopped fresh coriander (cilantro)
15ml/1 tbsp lemon juice
salt and ground black pepper
fried lemon wedges, to serve

1 Place the onion in a large pan with 300ml/ ½ pint/1 ¼ cups of the vegetable stock. Bring to the boil, lower the heat and simmer gently for about 10 minutes.

2 Meanwhile, spoon the cinnamon, turmeric, ginger and cayenne pepper into a bowl. Stir in 30ml/2 tbsp of the remaining stock to form a paste. Stir the spice paste into the onion mixture, together with the carrots and celery. Pour in the rest of the stock.

3 Bring the mixture to the boil, lower the heat, then cover and simmer gently for 5 minutes.

4 Stir in the tomatoes and potatoes. Cover and simmer gently for 20 minutes. Add the saffron, chickpeas, fresh coriander and lemon juice. Season to taste with salt and pepper. When piping hot, serve in heated bowls with fried lemon wedges.

Cook's Tip
Although it is very expensive, do not stint on the saffron, as it adds a unique flavour to the spice combination.

Lemon Oil Dip with Charred Artichokes

A tangy lemon and garlic dip makes the perfect accompaniment to roasted globe artichokes. It would also go well with barbecue-cooked baby artichokes.

Serves 4

15ml/1 tbsp lemon juice or white wine vinegar
2 globe artichokes, trimmed
12 garlic cloves, unpeeled
90ml/6 tbsp olive oil
1 lemon
sea salt
flat leaf parsley sprigs, to garnish

1 Preheat the oven to 200°C/400°F/Gas 6. Add the lemon juice or vinegar to a bowl of cold water. Cut each artichoke lengthways into wedges. Pull out and discard the hairy choke from the centre of each wedge, then drop the wedges into the acidulated water to prevent discoloration.

2 Drain the artichoke wedges and place them in a roasting pan with the garlic. Add half the olive oil and toss well to coat. Sprinkle with sea salt and roast for 40 minutes, stirring once or twice, until the artichokes are tender and a little charred.

3 Meanwhile, make the dip. Using a small, sharp knife, thinly pare away two strips of rind from the lemon. Lay the strips on a board and carefully scrape away any remaining pith. Place the rind in a small pan with water to cover. Bring to the boil, then simmer for 5 minutes. Drain the rind, refresh it in cold water, then chop it coarsely and set it aside.

4 Arrange the cooked artichokes on a serving plate and set them aside to cool for 5 minutes.

5 Press the garlic cloves to extract the flesh and put it in a bowl. Mash it to a purée, then add the lemon rind. Squeeze the juice from the lemon and whisk it into the garlic mixture. Finally, whisk in the remaining oil. Season with sea salt and serve with the warm artichokes. Garnish with flat leaf parsley.

Aioli with Fried Potato

Today, aioli is usually made in a food processor, rather than pounded with a pestle in a mortar, and is more like garlic mayonnaise.

Serves 4

vegetable oil, for deep-frying
4 potatoes, each cut into
    eight wedges
coarse sea salt

For the aioli

1 large (US extra large) egg yolk,
    at room temperature
5ml/1 tsp white wine vinegar
75ml/5 tbsp olive oil
75ml/5 tbsp sunflower oil
4 garlic cloves, crushed
parsley sprig, to garnish

1 First, make the aioli. Place the egg yolk and vinegar in a food processor. With the motor running, gradually add the olive oil, then the sunflower oil through the feeder tube, until the mixture has the consistency of a thick mayonnaise.

2 Scrape the mixture into a serving bowl and stir in the crushed garlic. Season with salt to taste, then cover closely and chill in the refrigerator until required.

3 Heat the vegetable oil in a large pan or deep-fryer to a temperature of 180°C/350°F or until a cube of day-old bread turns golden in about 60 seconds. Add the potato wedges and fry for about 7 minutes, until pale golden.

4 Lift out the potato wedges with a slotted spoon and drain them on kitchen paper. Increase the heat of the oil slightly, then return the potato wedges to the pan and fry them for a second time until crisp and golden brown. Remove with a slotted spoon and drain thoroughly on kitchen paper. Sprinkle with sea salt and serve hot with the aioli, garnished with parsley.

Cook's Tip
For an aioli with a milder flavour, use three parts sunflower oil to one part olive oil.

Mellow Garlic Dip

Two whole heads of garlic may seem like a lot but, once cooked, their flavour becomes sweet and mellow.

Serves 4
2 whole heads of garlic
15ml/1 tbsp olive oil

60ml/4 tbsp mayonnaise
75ml/5 tbsp Greek (US strained plain) yogurt
5ml/1 tsp wholegrain mustard
salt and ground black pepper
crunchy breadsticks, to serve (optional)

1 Preheat the oven to 200°C/400°F/Gas 6. Separate the garlic cloves and place them in a small roasting pan. Pour the olive oil over them and turn them with a spoon to coat evenly. Roast for 20–30 minutes, until tender and softened. Set aside to cool for 5 minutes.

2 Trim off the root end from each garlic clove, then peel. Place the garlic cloves on a chopping board and sprinkle with salt. Mash with a fork until puréed. Scrape the purée into a small bowl and stir in the mayonnaise, yogurt and mustard.

3 Check and adjust the seasoning, then spoon the dip into a serving bowl. Cover closely and chill until ready to serve.

Easy Garlic and Coconut Dip

This tastes fabulous with crudités or breadsticks.

Serves 4
5 garlic cloves
150g/5oz/2 cups dry grated coconut

30ml/2 tbsp chilli powder
150ml/¼ pint/⅔ cup natural (plain) yogurt
salt
crudités, to serve

1 Pound the garlic with a pinch of salt. Gradually work in the coconut and chilli powder to make a paste.
2 Stir the paste into the yogurt and serve with crudités.

Butternut Squash & Parmesan Dip

Butternut squash makes an unusual but very tasty dip, which is best served warm.

Serves 4
1 butternut squash
15g/½oz/1 tbsp butter

4 garlic cloves, unpeeled
30ml/2 tbsp freshly grated Parmesan cheese
45–75ml/3–5 tbsp double (heavy) cream
salt and ground black pepper
Melba toast, to serve

1 Preheat the oven to 200°C/400°F/Gas 6. Cut the butternut squash in half lengthways, then scoop out and discard the seeds. Use a small, sharp knife to score the flesh deeply in a criss-cross pattern; cut as close to the skin as possible, but take care not to cut through it.

2 Arrange both halves of the squash in a small roasting pan and dot them with the butter. Sprinkle with salt and pepper and roast for 20 minutes. Tuck the garlic cloves around the squash in the roasting pan. Bake for 20 minutes more, until the squash is tender and softened.

3 Scoop the flesh out of the squash shells and place it in a blender or food processor. Slip the garlic cloves out of their skins and add the pulp to the squash. Process until smooth.

4 With the motor running, add half the grated Parmesan cheese, then add the double cream. Check the seasoning. Spoon the dip into a serving bowl, sprinkle the reserved cheese over the top and serve the dip warm with Melba toast.

Cook's Tip
To make Melba toast, grill (broil) a slice of white bread on both sides until golden. Leave to cool slightly, then cut off and discard the crusts. Using a long, thin, very sharp knife, slice the bread in half horizontally to make two thinner slices. Toast the inner slices under the grill (broiler) until golden. Leave to cool, then store in an airtight container until required.

Tzatziki

Cool, creamy and refreshing, tzatziki is wonderfully easy to make and even easier to eat. Serve this classic Greek dip with pitta bread, potato wedges or a selection of chargrilled vegetables.

Serves 4

1 mini cucumber, trimmed
4 spring onions (scallions)
1 garlic clove
200ml/7fl oz/scant 1 cup Greek (US strained plain) yogurt
45ml/3 tbsp chopped fresh mint
salt and ground black pepper
fresh mint sprig, to garnish
toasted mini pitta breads, to serve

1 Cut the cucumber into 5mm/¼in dice. Trim the spring onions and garlic, then chop both very finely.

2 Beat the yogurt with a fork until smooth, if necessary, then gently stir in the diced cucumber, spring onions, garlic and chopped mint.

3 Scrape the mixture into a serving bowl and season with salt and plenty of ground black pepper to taste. Cover and chill in the refrigerator until needed. Garnish with a small mint sprig and serve with toasted mini pitta breads.

Cook's Tip
Choose Greek (US strained plain) yogurt for this dip – it has a higher fat content than most yogurts, which gives it a deliciously rich, creamy texture.

Variation
A similar, but smoother dip can be made in the food processor. Peel one mini cucumber and process with two garlic cloves and 75g/3oz/3 cups mixed fresh herbs to a purée. Stir the purée into 200ml/7fl oz/scant 1 cup sour cream and season to taste with salt and pepper.

Blue Cheese Dip

This dip can be mixed in next-to-no-time and is delicious served with ripe pears cut into wedges. If you add a little more yogurt to give a softer consistency, it makes a good salad dressing.

Serves 4

150g/5oz blue cheese, such as Stilton or Danish blue
150g/5oz/⅔ cup low-fat soft white (farmer's) cheese
about 75ml/5 tbsp Greek (US strained plain) yogurt
salt and ground black pepper

1 Crumble the blue cheese into a bowl. Using a wooden spoon, beat the cheese to soften it.

2 Add the soft white cheese and beat well to blend.

3 Gradually beat in the Greek yogurt, adding enough to give you the consistency you like.

4 Season with lots of black pepper and a little salt. Cover and chill in the refrigerator until ready to serve.

Sun-dried Tomato Swirl

Try this with celery sticks or carrot batons. It is also delicious as a topping on baked potatoes.

Serves 4

30ml/2 tbsp sun-dried tomato paste
250ml/8fl oz/1 cup Greek (US strained plain) yogurt
2 spring onions (scallions), finely chopped
2 sun-dried tomatoes in oil, drained and finely chopped
dash of Tabasco sauce (optional)
salt and ground black pepper

1 Mix the sun-dried tomato paste with a little of the yogurt until smooth, then gradually stir in the remaining yogurt.

2 Add the spring onions and chopped sun-dried tomatoes, season to taste with salt and pepper and mix well. If you like, spike the swirl with a dash of Tabasco.

Guacamole

One of the best-loved Mexican salsas, this blend of creamy avocado, tomatoes, garlic, chillies, coriander and lime now appears on tables the world over.

Serves 6–8

4 ripe avocados
juice of 1 lime
½ small onion
2 garlic cloves
small bunch of fresh coriander (cilantro), chopped
3 fresh red chillies
4 tomatoes, peeled, seeded and coarsely chopped
salt
tortilla chips, to serve

1 Cut the avocados in half and remove the stones (pits). Scoop the flesh out of the shells and place it in a food processor or blender. Process until almost smooth, then scrape into a bowl and stir in the lime juice. For a chunkier dip, mash the avocado flesh coarsely with a fork.

2 Chop the onion finely, then crush the garlic. Add both to the avocado and mix well. Stir in the coriander.

3 Remove the stalks from the chillies, slit the pods and scrape out the seeds with a small sharp knife. Chop the chillies finely and add them to the avocado mixture, together with the chopped tomatoes. Mix well.

4 Check the seasoning and add salt to taste. Cover closely with clear film (plastic wrap) or a tight-fitting lid and chill for 1 hour before serving as a dip with tortilla chips.

> **Cook's Tips**
> • *If it is well covered, guacamole will keep in the refrigerator for 2–3 days, but it will tend to turn greyish.*
> • *Submerging an avocado stone in the guacamole is said to inhibit discoloration.*
> • *Traditionally, avocados are cut with a silver-bladed knife – again to prevent discoloration.*

Aubergine & Pepper Spread

With its rich colour and robust texture, this mixture makes an excellent contrast to a creamy cheese dip. It goes especially well with black olives.

Serves 6–8

2 aubergines (eggplant), total weight about 675g/1½lb, halved lengthways
2 green (bell) peppers, seeded and quartered
45ml/3 tbsp olive oil
2 firm ripe tomatoes, halved, seeded and finely chopped
45ml/3 tbsp chopped fresh parsley or coriander (cilantro)
2 garlic cloves, crushed
30ml/2 tbsp red wine vinegar
lemon juice, to taste
salt and ground black pepper
fresh parsley or coriander sprigs, to garnish
dark rye bread, lemon wedges and black olives, to serve

1 Place the aubergines and pepper quarters, skin side up, on a grill (broiler) rack and grill (broil) until the skins have blistered and charred. Turn the vegetables over and cook for 3 minutes more. Transfer to a bowl, cover with crumpled kitchen paper and leave to cool for about 10 minutes.

2 Peel away the blackened skin. Place the aubergine and pepper flesh in a food processor and process to a purée.

3 With the motor running, pour in the olive oil in a continuous stream through the feeder tube and process until smooth and thoroughly combined.

4 Scrape the mixture into a serving bowl and stir in the chopped tomatoes, parsley or coriander, garlic, vinegar and lemon juice. Season to taste with salt and pepper, garnish with the parsley or coriander sprigs and serve with dark rye bread, wedges of lemon and black olives.

> **Cook's Tip**
> *This dip is delicious served with any rustic bread, such as olive bread or ciabatta.*

Eggs in Baked Potatoes

Nestled in creamy baked potatoes, cheese-topped eggs make a substantial, nourishing and inexpensive snack for all the family.

Serves 4
4 large baking potatoes
40g/1½oz/3 tbsp butter

30ml/2 tbsp hot single (light)
   cream or milk
30ml/2 tbsp chopped fresh chives
4 eggs
about 50g/2oz/½ cup finely
   grated mature (sharp)
   Cheddar cheese
salt and ground black pepper
celery sticks and chives, to garnish

1 Preheat the oven to 200°C/400°F/Gas 6. Prick the potatoes with a fork and bake for 1–1¼ hours, until soft.

2 Working quickly, cut a slice about a quarter to a third of the way down from the top of each potato, then scoop the flesh into a bowl with a teaspoon, taking care not to pierce the potato skins. Reserve the skins.

3 Add the butter and cream or milk to the potato flesh, together with the chives. Season to taste with salt and pepper. Mash the ingredients together.

4 Divide the potato mixture among the potato skins, and make a hollow in each with the back of a spoon.

5 Break an egg into each hollow, season to taste with salt and pepper, then return to the oven for about 10 minutes, until the eggs are just set.

6 Sprinkle the cheese over the eggs, then place under a hot grill (broiler) until golden. Serve, garnished with celery and chives.

Cook's Tip
Bake the potatoes in the microwave, if you prefer. For crisp skins, pop them into a preheated 200°C/400°F/Gas 6 oven for about 10 minutes after microwave cooking.

Potato Pancakes

Crisp on the outside, with tender centres, these potato pancakes are delicious with sour cream and a salad.

Serves 6–8
6 large waxy potatoes, peeled
2 eggs, beaten
1–2 garlic cloves, crushed
115g/4oz/1 cup plain (all-
   purpose) flour

5ml/1 tsp chopped
   fresh marjoram
50g/2oz/¼ cup butter
60ml/4 tbsp vegetable oil
salt and ground black pepper

To serve
sour cream
chopped fresh parsley
tomato salad

1 Coarsely grate the potatoes on to a clean dishtowel, then gather up the sides and squeeze tightly to remove as much moisture as possible.

2 Tip the potatoes into a bowl and add the beaten eggs, garlic, flour and marjoram. Season to taste with salt and pepper and mix well.

3 Heat half the butter and half the oil in a large frying pan, then add large spoonfuls of the potato mixture to form rounds. Using the back of a dampened spoon, carefully flatten the rounds into pancakes.

4 Fry the pancakes until crisp and golden brown, then turn them over carefully and cook on the other side. Drain on kitchen paper and keep hot while cooking the rest of the pancakes, adding the remaining butter and oil to the frying pan as necessary.

5 Serve the pancakes topped with sour cream, sprinkled with parsley, and accompanied by a fresh, juicy tomato salad.

Cook's Tip
Choose firm-fleshed potatoes, such as Charlotte or Kipfler.

Idaho Potato Slices

This dish is made from layered potatoes, cheese and herbs. Cooking the ingredients together gives them a very rich flavour.

Serves 4
3 large potatoes
butter, for greasing
1 small onion, thinly sliced
 into rings

200g/7oz/1¾ cups grated
 Red Leicester or mature (sharp)
 Cheddar cheese
fresh thyme sprigs
150ml/¼ pint/⅔ cup single
 (light) cream
salt and ground black pepper
salad leaves, to serve

1 Preheat the oven to 200°C/400°F/Gas 6. Peel the potatoes and cook them in a large pan of lightly salted boiling water for 10 minutes, until they are just starting to soften. Remove from the water and pat dry.

2 Slice the potatoes thinly, using the straight edge of a grater or a mandoline. Grease the base and sides of an 18cm/7in cake tin (pan) with butter and lay some of the potatoes on the base to cover it completely. Season to taste with salt and pepper.

3 Sprinkle some of the onion rings over the potatoes and top with a little of the grated cheese. Sprinkle over some thyme leaves. Continue to layer the ingredients, finishing with a layer of cheese. Season to taste with salt and pepper. Press the potato layers right down. (The mixture may seem quite high at this point, but it will cook down.)

4 Pour the cream over and bake for 35–45 minutes. Remove from the oven and cool. Invert on to a plate and cut into wedges. Serve with a few salad leaves.

Variation
If you want to make this snack more substantial, top the wedges with grilled (broiled) red (bell) peppers.

Potato Skins with Cajun Dip

Divinely crisp and naughty, these potato skins taste great with this piquant dip.

Serves 2
2 large baking potatoes
vegetable oil, for deep-frying

For the dip
120ml/4fl oz/½ cup natural
 (plain) yogurt
1 garlic clove, crushed
5ml/1 tsp tomato purée (paste)
2.5ml/½ tsp green chilli purée
 (paste) or ½ small fresh green
 chilli, chopped
1.5ml/¼ tsp celery salt
pinch of cayenne
 pepper (optional)
salt and ground black pepper

1 Preheat the oven to 180°C/350°F/Gas 4. Prick the potatoes and bake for 1–1¼ hours, until tender. Cut them in half and scoop out the flesh, leaving a thin layer on the skins. Keep the flesh for another meal.

2 Meanwhile, make the dip. Mix the yogurt, garlic, tomato purée, chilli purée or fresh chilli and celery salt in a bowl. Season to taste with cayenne, if using, salt and pepper. Cover with clear film (plastic wrap) and chill in the refrigerator.

3 Pour vegetable oil to a depth of about 1cm/½in into a large pan or deep-fat fryer. Heat to 180°C/350°F or until a cube of day-old bread turns golden brown in about 60 seconds. Cut each potato-skin half in half again, then fry them until crisp and golden on both sides.

4 Drain the fried potato skins on kitchen paper, sprinkle with salt and black pepper and serve with a bowl of dip or with a spoonful of dip in each skin.

Cook's Tip
If you like, you can microwave the potatoes to save time. On the maximum setting, this will take about 10 minutes.

Samosas

These are far too good to
be served only as cocktail
party nibbles. Enjoy them
for lunches or snacks, too.

Makes about 20
1 packet 25cm/10in square
   spring roll wrappers, thawed
   if frozen
30ml/2 tbsp plain (all-purpose)
   flour, mixed to a paste with
   water
vegetable oil, for deep-frying
fresh coriander (cilantro) leaves,
   to garnish

For the filling
25g/1oz/2 tbsp ghee
1 small onion, finely chopped
1cm/½in piece of fresh root
   ginger, chopped
1 garlic clove, crushed
2.5ml/½ tsp chilli powder
225g/8oz potato, cooked until just
   tender, then finely diced
50g/2oz/½ cup cauliflower
   florets, lightly cooked, chopped
50g/2oz/½ cup frozen peas,
   thawed
5–10ml/1–2 tsp garam masala
15ml/1 tbsp chopped fresh
   coriander
squeeze of lemon juice
salt

1 To make the filling, heat the ghee in a large wok or frying pan
and cook the onion, ginger and garlic for 5 minutes, until the
onion has softened but not browned. Stir in the chilli powder
and cook for 1 minute, then add the potato, cauliflower and
peas. Mix well. Sprinkle with garam masala and set aside to
cool. Stir in the chopped coriander, lemon juice and salt.

2 Cut the spring roll wrappers into three strips. Brush the
edges with a little of the flour paste. Place a small spoonful of
filling about 2cm/¾in from the edge of one strip. Fold one
corner over it to make a triangle and continue this folding until
the entire strip has been used and a triangular pastry has been
formed. Seal any open edges with more flour and water paste.

3 Heat the oil for deep-frying to 180°C/350°F or until a cube
of day-old bread turns golden brown in 60 seconds. Fry the
samosas, a few at a time, until golden and crisp. Drain well on
kitchen paper and keep hot while you cook the remaining
batches. Serve hot, garnished with coriander leaves.

Spinach Empanadillas

These little Spanish pastry
turnovers are filled with
ingredients that have a
strong Moorish influence –
pine nuts and raisins.

Makes 20
25g/1oz/3 tbsp raisins
25ml/1½ tbsp olive oil
450g/1lb fresh young
   spinach, chopped

2 garlic cloves, finely chopped
25g/1oz/⅓ cup pine
   nuts, chopped
350g/12oz puff pastry, thawed
   if frozen
butter, for greasing
1 egg, beaten, to glaze
salt and ground black pepper

1 Put the raisins in bowl and pour over sufficient warm water
to cover. Set aside to soak for 10 minutes. Drain thoroughly,
then chop coarsely.

2 Heat the oil in a large sauté pan or wok. Add the spinach, stir,
then cover and cook over a low heat for about 2 minutes.

3 Take the lid off the pan, turn up the heat and let any liquid
evaporate. Add the garlic and season with plenty of salt and
pepper. Cook, stirring constantly, for 1 minute more. Remove
the pan from the heat, stir in the raisins and pine nuts and set
aside to cool.

4 Preheat the oven to 180°C/350°F/Gas 4. Roll out the pastry
thinly. Using a 7.5cm/3in pastry (cookie) cutter, stamp out
20 rounds, re rolling the dough if necessary.

5 Place about 10ml/2 tsp of the filling in the middle of a round,
then brush the edges with a little water. Bring up the sides
of the pastry and seal well to make a turnover. Press the edges
together with the back of a fork. Make more turnovers in the
same way.

6 Place the turnovers on a lightly greased baking sheet, brush
with the beaten egg and bake for about 15 minutes, until
golden. Serve warm.

Mexican Tortilla Parcels

Seeded green chillies add just a flicker of fire to the spicy filling in these parcels.

Serves 4
60ml/4 tbsp sunflower oil
1 large onion, thinly sliced
1 garlic clove, crushed
10ml/2 tsp cumin seeds
2 fresh green chillies, seeded and chopped
675g/1½lb tomatoes, peeled and chopped
30ml/2 tbsp tomato purée (paste)
1 vegetable stock cube
200g/7oz can corn kernels, drained
15ml/1 tbsp chopped fresh coriander (cilantro)
115g/4oz/1 cup grated Cheddar cheese
12 wheat flour tortillas
fresh coriander leaves, shredded lettuce and sour cream, to serve
1 fresh red chilli, sliced, to garnish

1 Heat half the oil in a frying pan and cook the onion with the garlic and cumin seeds for 5 minutes, until the onion softens. Add the chillies and tomatoes, then stir in the tomato purée.

2 Crumble the stock cube over, stir well and cook gently for 5 minutes, until the chilli is soft but the tomatoes have not broken down completely. Stir in the corn and fresh coriander and heat gently to warm through. Keep hot.

3 Sprinkle grated cheese in the middle of each tortilla. Spoon some tomato mixture over the cheese. Fold over one edge of the tortilla, then the sides and finally the remaining edge to enclose the filling completely.

4 Heat the remaining oil in a frying pan and fry the filled tortillas for 1–2 minutes on each side, until crisp. Garnish with chillies and serve with coriander, lettuce and sour cream.

> **Cook's Tip**
> *Mexican wheat flour tortillas are available in most supermarkets. Keep them in the cupboard as instant wraps for a variety of vegetable and cheese mixtures.*

Spiced Sweet Potato Turnovers

A subtle hint of sweetness underscores the spicy flavour of these pastries.

beaten egg, to glaze
salt and ground black pepper
fresh mint sprigs, to garnish

Serves 4
15ml/1 tbsp olive oil
1 small (US medium) egg
150ml/¼ pint/⅔ cup natural (plain) yogurt
115g/4oz/½ cup butter, melted
275g/10oz/2½ cups plain (all-purpose) flour
1.5ml/¼ tsp bicarbonate of soda (baking soda)
10ml/2 tsp paprika

For the filling
1 sweet potato, about 225g/8oz
30ml/2 tbsp vegetable oil
2 shallots, finely chopped
10ml/2 tsp coriander seeds, crushed
5ml/1 tsp ground cumin
5ml/1 tsp garam masala
115g/4oz/1 cup frozen petits pois, thawed
15ml/1 tbsp chopped fresh mint

1 To make the filling, cook the sweet potato in boiling salted water for 15–20 minutes, until tender. Drain and leave to cool, then peel the potato and cut into 1cm/½in cubes.

2 Heat the vegetable oil in a frying pan and cook the shallots until softened. Add the potato and cook until it browns at the edges. Sprinkle over the spices and cook, stirring, for a few seconds. Remove the pan from the heat and add the peas and mint and season with salt and pepper to taste. Leave to cool.

3 Preheat the oven to 200°C/400°F/Gas 6. Grease a baking sheet. To make the pastry, whisk the oil with the egg, stir in the yogurt, then the melted butter. Sift the flour, soda, paprika and 5ml/1 tsp salt into a bowl, then stir into the yogurt mixture.

4 Turn out the dough, and knead gently. Roll it out, then stamp out 10cm/4in rounds. Spoon 10ml/2 tsp of the filling on to one side of each round, fold over and seal the edges. Re-roll the trimmings and stamp out more rounds until the filling is used.

5 Arrange the turnovers on the baking sheet and brush with beaten egg. Bake for 20 minutes, until crisp. Garnish and serve.

Falafel

In North Africa, these spicy fritters are made using dried broad (fava) beans, but chickpeas are much easier to buy. They are lovely served as a snack with creamy yogurt or stuffed into warmed pitta bread.

Serves 4

150g/5oz/ ⅔ cup dried
   chickpeas
1 large onion, coarsely chopped
2 garlic cloves, coarsely chopped
60ml/4 tbsp coarsely
   chopped parsley
5ml/1 tsp cumin seeds, crushed
5ml/1 tsp coriander
   seeds, crushed
2.5ml/ ½ tsp baking powder
vegetable oil, for deep-frying
salt and ground black pepper

To serve

pitta bread
salad
natural (plain) yogurt

1 Put the chickpeas in a bowl with plenty of cold water. Leave to soak overnight.

2 Drain the chickpeas and put them in a large pan. Pour over enough water to cover them by at least 5cm/2in. Bring to the boil. Boil rapidly for 10 minutes, then lower the heat and simmer for 1–1½ hours, until soft.

3 Drain the chickpeas and place them in a food processor. Add the onion, garlic, parsley, cumin seeds, coriander seeds and baking powder. Season with salt and pepper to taste. Process until the mixture forms a fine paste.

4 As soon as the paste is cool enough to handle, shape it into walnut-size balls, flattening them slightly.

5 Pour oil to a depth of 5cm/2in into a deep frying pan. Heat until a little of the falafel mixture added to the hot oil sizzles on the surface.

6 Fry the falafel, in batches, until golden. Drain on kitchen paper and keep hot while frying the remainder. Serve warm in pitta bread, with salad and yogurt.

Courgettes, Carrots & Pecans in Pitta Bread

Easy to eat and very tasty, this makes a good, healthy after-school snack or a nourishing light lunch.

Serves 2

2 carrots
25g/1oz/ ¼ cup pecan nuts
4 spring onions (scallions), sliced
45ml/3 tbsp olive oil
60ml/4 tbsp Greek (US strained
   plain) yogurt
5ml/1 tsp lemon juice
15ml/1 tbsp chopped fresh mint
2 courgettes (zucchini)
25g/1oz/ ¼ cup plain (all-
   purpose) flour
2 pitta breads
salt and ground black pepper
shredded lettuce, to serve

1 Trim the carrots. Grate them coarsely into a bowl. Stir in the pecans and spring onions and toss well.

2 In a clean bowl, whisk 7.5ml/ 1½ tsp of the olive oil with the yogurt, lemon juice and the fresh mint. Stir the dressing into the carrot mixture and mix thoroughly. Cover and chill in the refrigerator until required.

3 Trim the courgettes. Cut them diagonally into fairly thin slices. Season the flour with a little salt and pepper. Spread it out on a plate and coat the courgette slices. Shake off any excess flour.

4 Heat the remaining oil in a large frying pan. Add the coated courgette slices and cook for 3–4 minutes, turning once, until browned. Drain the courgettes on kitchen paper.

5 Make a slit in each pitta bread to form a pocket. Fill the pittas with the carrot mixture and the courgette slices. Serve immediately on a bed of shredded lettuce.

> **Cook's Tip**
> Warm the pitta breads, if you like. Do not fill them too soon or the carrot mixture will make the bread soggy.

QUICK & EASY

Even people who love to cook know there are times when only fast food will do – and, sadly, this is sometimes at the expense of flavour, quality and nutritional value. But no more – this chapter is the answer to the busy vegetarian cook's prayer. It is packed with fabulous recipes that can be made and cooked in minutes, yet use fresh ingredients and taste wonderful. There is something to suit all tastes and ages from creamy pasta dishes to filling frittatas and from spicy curries to tasty toast toppers.

When you are in a rush or simply not in the mood for cooking, the most difficult thing is often deciding what to eat. This collection of imaginative ideas resolves the problem. Why settle for a boring cheese sandwich when, in the time it would take to butter the bread and slice the cheese, you can produce a light and fluffy Classic Cheese Omelette? In very little longer, you can liven up tired old taste buds with Spiced Tofu Stir-fry, or rustle up Crispy Noodles with Mixed Vegetables as an after-school treat for hungry children. Quick-cooked dishes are ideal for busy families whose individual members never seem to be at home at the same time. With these irresistible recipes, you can be sure that your family is eating a healthy diet without feeling as if you are running a restaurant, as single servings can be ready in the wink of an eye.

Herb Omelette

It takes only moments to make a simple, herb-flavoured omelette. Serve it with a salad and a chunk of crusty bread and it becomes a nutritious light meal.

Serves 1
2 eggs
15ml/1 tbsp chopped fresh herbs, such as parsley or chives
5ml/1 tsp butter
salt and ground black pepper
fresh parsley, to garnish

1 Lightly beat the eggs in a bowl, add the fresh herbs and season to taste with salt and pepper.

2 Melt the butter in a heavy omelette pan or non-stick frying pan and swirl it around to coat the base evenly.

3 Keeping the heat fairly high, pour in the egg mixture. Let it start to set for 1–2 minutes, then lower the heat. Using a spoon or spatula, lift the edges of the omelette and push them gently towards the centre, so that the raw egg runs in to fill the gap, then starts to set as well.

4 Cook for about 2 minutes, without stirring, until the omelette is lightly set. Quickly fold it over and slide on to a plate. Serve immediately, garnished with parsley.

Cook's Tips
• It is important to serve omelettes as soon as they are cooked, so this is one occasion when it would be unrealistic to expect everyone to be served simultaneously. Seat your guests and serve each omelette as soon as it is cooked.
• Omelettes have an undeserved reputation for being difficult to make. There are two secrets to success. A good-quality, heavy omelette or frying pan makes sure that there is an even distribution of heat throughout the base. It is essential to be sure that the butter has melted completely and to swirl it around so the entire base of the pan is evenly coated before adding the beaten egg mixture.

Classic Cheese Omelette

Perhaps the ultimate fast food – a couple of eggs, some well-flavoured cheese, a pat of butter and a good pan and you soon have a satisfying meal.

Serves 1
2 large (US extra large) eggs
15ml/1 tbsp chopped fresh herbs, such as chives, parsley or dill
5ml/1 tsp butter
50g/2oz/ 1/2 cup grated full-flavoured cheese, such as Gruyère, Gouda or Cheddar
salt and ground black pepper
fresh flat leaf parsley, to garnish
tomato wedges, to serve

1 Lightly beat the eggs in a bowl and quickly mix in the herbs. Season to taste with salt and pepper.

2 Melt the butter in a 20cm/8in heavy omelette pan or non-stick frying pan, swirling it around to coat the base evenly.

3 Keeping the heat fairly high, pour in the egg mixture. Let it set for 1–2 minutes, then lower the heat. Using a spoon or spatula, lift the edges of the omelette and push them gently towards the centre, so that the raw egg runs in to fill the gap, then starts to set as well.

4 When the egg at the sides is firm, but the centre remains soft, sprinkle over the cheese. Leave undisturbed to cook for about 30 seconds.

5 Fold the edge of the omelette nearest the handle over, then roll it over on to a warmed plate. Serve immediately with a garnish of fresh flat leaf parsley and tomato wedges.

Variation
You can add other ingredients to the cheese. Crunchy, garlic-flavoured croûtons are good, as are sautéed sliced mushrooms or chopped tomatoes.

Potato & Onion Tortilla

One of the signature dishes of Spain, this delicious thick potato and onion omelette is eaten at all times of the day, hot or cold.

Serves 4

300ml/ ½ pint/ 1 ¼ cups olive oil
6 large potatoes, sliced
2 Spanish onions, sliced
6 large (US extra large) eggs
salt and ground black pepper
cherry tomatoes, halved, to serve

1 Heat the oil in a large non-stick frying pan. Stir in the potato and onion slices and a little salt. Cover and cook gently for 20 minutes, until soft.

2 Beat the eggs. Transfer the onion and potato slices to the eggs with a slotted spoon. Season to taste. Pour off some of the oil from the frying pan, leaving about 60ml/4 tbsp.

3 When the oil is very hot, pour in the egg mixture. Cook for 2–3 minutes. Cover the pan with a plate, then, holding them together, invert the tortilla on to the plate. Slide it back into the pan and cook for 5 minutes more. Serve with the tomatoes.

Pasta Frittata

This is a great way to use up cold leftover pasta.

Serves 4

225g/8oz cold cooked pasta, with any sauce

50g/2oz/⅔ cup freshly grated Parmesan cheese
5 eggs, lightly beaten
65g/2½oz/5 tbsp butter
salt and ground black pepper

1 Stir the pasta and Parmesan into the eggs. Season to taste.
2 Heat half the butter in a large pan. Pour in the egg mixture and cook for 4–5 minutes, gently shaking the pan.
3 Place a plate over the pan, then, holding them together, invert the frittata on to the plate. Melt the remaining butter in the pan, slide the frittata back in and cook for 3–4 minutes more.

Sweet Pepper & Courgette Frittata

Eggs, cheese and vegetables form the basis of this excellent supper dish. Served cold, in wedges, it makes tasty picnic fare too.

Serves 4
45ml/3 tbsp olive oil
1 red onion, thinly sliced
1 large red (bell) pepper, seeded and thinly sliced

1 large yellow (bell) pepper, seeded and thinly sliced
2 garlic cloves, crushed
1 medium courgette (zucchini), thinly sliced
6 eggs
150g/5oz/1 ¼ cups grated Italian cheese, such as Fontina
salt and ground black pepper
dressed mixed salad leaves, to serve

1 Heat 30ml/2 tbsp of the olive oil in a large heavy frying pan that can safely be used under the grill (broiler). (Cover a wooden handle with foil to protect it.) Add the onion and red and yellow pepper slices and cook over a low heat, stirring occasionally, for about 10 minutes, until softened.

2 Add the remaining oil to the pan. When it is hot, add the garlic and the courgette slices. Cook over a low heat, stirring constantly, for 5 minutes.

3 Beat the eggs with salt and pepper to taste. Stir in the grated cheese. Pour the mixture over the vegetables, stirring lightly to mix. Cook over a low heat until the mixture is just set.

4 Meanwhile, preheat the grill. When it is hot, slide the pan underneath and brown the top of the frittata lightly. Let the frittata stand in the pan for about 5 minutes before cutting into wedges. Serve hot or cold, with the salad.

> **Cook's Tips**
> • When adding the egg mixture to the vegetables, make sure that it covers the base of the pan evenly.
> • Make sure that you use the freshest possible free-range (farm-fresh) eggs for maximum flavour.

Creamy Cannellini Beans with Asparagus

In this tasty toast topper, cannellini beans in a creamy sauce contrast with tender asparagus spears.

Serves 2

10ml/2 tsp butter
1 small onion, finely chopped
1 small carrot, grated
5ml/1 tsp fresh thyme leaves

400g/14oz can cannellini
 beans, drained
150ml/ 1/4 pint/ 2/3 cup
 single (light) cream
115g/4oz young asparagus
 spears, trimmed
2 slices Granary (multigrain)
 bread
salt and ground black pepper

1 Melt the butter in a pan. Add the onion and carrot and cook over a moderate heat, stirring occasionally, for 4 minutes, until soft. Add the thyme leaves.

2 Rinse the cannellini beans in a sieve under cold running water. Drain, then add to the onion and carrot. Mix lightly.

3 Pour in the cream and heat slowly to just below boiling point, stirring occasionally. Remove the pan from the heat and season with salt and pepper to taste.

4 Place the asparagus spears in a pan. Pour over just enough boiling water to cover. Poach for 3–4 minutes, until the spears are just tender.

5 Meanwhile, toast the bread under a hot grill (broiler) until both sides are golden. Place the toast on individual plates. Drain the asparagus and divide the spears between the slices of toast. Spoon the bean mixture over each portion and serve.

> **Variation**
> *Try making this with other canned beans, such as borlotti, haricot (navy) or flageolet (small cannellini).*

Parsley, Lemon & Garlic Mushrooms on Toast

Don't overwhelm the delicate flavour of wild mushrooms by adding too much garlic. Temper the taste with sherry, parsley and lemon juice.

Serves 4

25g/1oz/2 tbsp butter, plus extra
 for spreading
1 medium onion, chopped

1 garlic clove, crushed
350g/12oz/4¾ cups assorted
 wild mushrooms, sliced
45ml/3 tbsp dry sherry
75ml/5 tbsp chopped fresh flat
 leaf parsley
15ml/1 tbsp lemon juice
salt and ground black pepper
4 slices brown or white bread

1 Melt the butter in a large non-stick frying pan. Add the onion and cook over a low heat, stirring occasionally, for 5 minutes without letting it colour.

2 Add the garlic and mushrooms, cover and cook over a medium heat for 3–5 minutes. Stir in the sherry and cook, uncovered, until all the liquid has been absorbed.

3 Stir in the parsley and lemon juice and then season to taste with salt and pepper.

4 Toast the bread, spread it with butter and place each piece on a serving plate. Spoon the mushroom mixture over the toast and serve immediately.

> **Cook's Tips**
> • *Flat leaf parsley, also known as Italian parsley, has a good flavour and keeps well in the refrigerator. To keep it fresh, stand the bunch in a jar of water and cover with a plastic bag.*
> • *Use any mixture of wild mushrooms, such as field mushrooms, horse mushrooms and shaggy ink caps or, more economically, a mixture of wild and cultivated mushrooms.*

Quorn with Ginger, Chilli & Leeks

If you've never eaten Quorn, this would be a good recipe to try. Serve it over noodles or rice.

Serves 4

45ml/3 tbsp soy sauce
30ml/2 tbsp dry sherry
  or vermouth
225g/8oz/2 cups Quorn
  (mycoprotein) cubes
10ml/2 tsp clear honey
150ml/ ¼ pint/ ⅔ cup
  Vegetable Stock
10ml/2 tsp cornflour (cornstarch)
45ml/3 tbsp sunflower oil
3 leeks, thinly sliced
1 fresh red chilli, seeded
  and sliced
2.5cm/1in piece of fresh root
  ginger, shredded
salt and ground black pepper

1 Mix the soy sauce and sherry or vermouth in a bowl. Add the Quorn cubes, toss until well coated and leave to marinate for about 30 minutes.

2 Using a slotted spoon, lift out the Quorn cubes from the marinade and set them aside. Stir the honey, stock and cornflour into the remaining marinade to make a paste.

3 Heat the oil in a wok. When it is hot, stir-fry the Quorn cubes until they are crisp on the outside. Remove the Quorn and set aside.

4 Reheat the oil and stir-fry the leeks, chilli and ginger for about 2 minutes, until they are just soft. Season lightly.

5 Add the Quorn cubes to the vegetables in the wok and mix well. Stir the marinade mixture, pour it into the wok and stir until it forms a thick, glossy coating for the Quorn and vegetables. Serve immediately.

> **Cook's Tip**
> Quorn is a versatile mycoprotein food, which easily absorbs different flavours and retains a good firm texture. It is available from most supermarkets.

Spiced Tofu Stir-fry

Like Quorn, firm tofu is a boon to the vegetarian cook, as it readily absorbs the flavours of the other ingredients. In this recipe, it is coated with warm spices before being stir-fried with a medley of mixed vegetables.

Serves 4

10ml/2 tsp ground cumin
15ml/1 tbsp paprika
5ml/1 tsp ground ginger
good pinch of cayenne pepper
15ml/1 tbsp caster
  (superfine) sugar
275g/10oz tofu, cubed
30ml/2 tbsp vegetable oil
2 garlic cloves, crushed
1 bunch spring onions
  (scallions), sliced
1 red (bell) pepper, seeded
  and sliced
1 yellow (bell) pepper, seeded
  and sliced
225g/8oz/3¼ cups brown cap
  (cremini) mushrooms, halved
1 large courgette (zucchini), sliced
115g/4oz/1 cup fine green
  beans, halved
50g/2oz/ ½ cup pine nuts
15ml/1 tbsp lime juice
15ml/1 tbsp clear honey
salt and ground black pepper

1 Mix the cumin, paprika, ginger, cayenne and sugar in a bowl and add plenty of salt and pepper. Coat the tofu cubes in the spice mixture.

2 Heat 15ml/1 tbsp of the vegetable oil in a wok or large, heavy frying pan and cook the tofu cubes over a high heat for 3–4 minutes, turning occasionally and taking care not to break them up too much. Remove the tofu cubes with a slotted spoon and drain on kitchen paper. Wipe out the pan with kitchen paper and return it to the heat.

3 Heat the remaining oil in the wok and stir-fry the garlic and spring onions for 3 minutes. Add the red and yellow peppers, mushrooms, courgette and beans and toss over a medium heat for about 6 minutes, or until beginning to soften and turn golden. Season well with salt and pepper.

4 Return the tofu cubes to the wok and add the pine nuts, lime juice and honey. Heat through, lightly stirring occasionally, then serve immediately.

Spiced Coconut Mushrooms

These delicious mushrooms can be served with almost any vegetarian meal, and are also good as a toast topping.

Serves 3–4
30ml/2 tbsp groundnut (peanut) oil
2 fresh red chillies, seeded and sliced into rings

2 garlic cloves, finely chopped
3 shallots, finely chopped
225g/8oz/3¼ cups brown cap (cremini) mushrooms, thickly sliced
150ml/¼ pint/⅔ cup coconut milk
30ml/2 tbsp chopped fresh coriander (cilantro)
salt and ground black pepper

1 Heat the oil in a wok, add the chillies and garlic, then stir-fry for a few seconds. Add the shallots and stir-fry for 2–3 minutes, until softened. Add the mushrooms and cook for 3 minutes.

2 Pour in the coconut milk and bring to the boil. Boil rapidly until the liquid is reduced by half and coats the mushrooms. Season to taste with salt and pepper. Sprinkle over the chopped coriander and toss gently to mix. Serve immediately.

Pickled Mushrooms

Add a little olive oil to the liquid when serving these spicy mushrooms.

Makes 1 jar
250ml/8fl oz/1 cup white wine vinegar
150ml/¼ pint/⅔ cup water

5ml/1 tsp salt
1 fresh red chilli
10ml/2 tsp coriander seeds
10ml/2 tsp black peppercorns
225g/8oz/3¼ cups firm button (white) mushrooms

1 Pour the vinegar and water into a stainless steel pan. Bring to simmering point, add the remaining ingredients and cook for 10 minutes.
2 Pour into a hot sterilized jar. Seal, label and leave to cool. Store in the refrigerator for at least 10 days before opening.

Sprouting Beans & Pak Choi

Health-food stores are a good source of the more unusual sprouting beans, or you can sprout your own.

Serves 4
45ml/3 tbsp groundnut (peanut) oil
3 spring onions (scallions), sliced
2 garlic cloves, cut in slivers
2.5cm/1in piece of fresh root ginger, cut in slivers
1 carrot, cut in thin sticks
150g/5oz/1¼ cups sprouting beans

200g/7oz pak choi (bok choy), shredded
50g/2oz/½ cup unsalted cashew nuts or halved almonds

For the sauce
45ml/3 tbsp light soy sauce
30ml/2 tbsp dry sherry
15ml/1 tbsp sesame oil
15ml/1 tbsp chilli sauce
150ml/¼ pint/⅔ cup cold water
5ml/1 tsp cornflour (cornstarch)
5ml/1 tsp clear honey
ground black pepper

1 Heat the oil in a large wok and stir-fry the onions, garlic, ginger and carrot for 2 minutes. Add the sprouting beans and stir-fry for 2 minutes more, stirring and tossing them together.

2 Add the pak choi and cashew nuts or almonds. Toss over the heat for 2–3 minutes, until the cabbage leaves are just wilting.

3 Quickly mix all the sauce ingredients in a jug (pitcher) and pour the sauce into the wok, stirring constantly until it is hot and coats the vegetables. Season to taste with pepper and serve immediately.

Cook's Tip
To sprout your own beans, soak dried mung beans, soya beans, lentils, aduki beans or chickpeas overnight in cold water. Drain and place in a large glass jar, filling it no more than one-sixth full. Pour in cold water and cover with muslin (cheesecloth), kept in place by an elastic band. Pour away the water, so that the beans are just damp, and put the jar in a cool, dark place. Rinse daily. You should have edible sprouts in 5–6 days.

Vegetable Korma

The blending of spices is an ancient art in India. Here the aim is to produce a subtle, aromatic curry.

Serves 4
50g/2oz/ ¼ cup butter
2 onions, sliced
2 garlic cloves, crushed
2.5cm/1 in piece of fresh root
 ginger, grated
5ml/1 tsp ground cumin
15ml/1 tbsp ground coriander
6 cardamom pods
5cm/2in piece of cinnamon stick
5ml/1 tsp ground turmeric
1 fresh red chilli, seeded and
 finely chopped
1 potato, cut into 2.5cm/
 1in cubes
1 small aubergine
 (eggplant), chopped
115g/4oz/1²⁄₃ cups mushrooms,
 thickly sliced
175ml/6fl oz/¾ cup water
115g/4oz green beans, cut into
 short lengths
60ml/4 tbsp natural (plain) yogurt
150ml/ ¼ pint/ ²⁄₃ cup double
 (heavy) cream
5ml/1 tsp garam masala
salt and ground black pepper
fresh coriander (cilantro) sprigs, to
 garnish
poppadums, to serve

1 Melt the butter in a pan and cook the onions for 5 minutes, until soft. Add the garlic and ginger and cook for 2 minutes, then stir in the cumin, ground coriander, cardamoms, cinnamon, turmeric and chilli. Stir-fry for 30 seconds.

2 Add the potato, aubergine, mushrooms and water. Cover the pan, bring to the boil, then lower the heat and simmer for 15 minutes. Add the beans and cook, uncovered, for 5 minutes.

3 Transfer the vegetables to a warmed serving dish. Boil the cooking liquid until reduced. Season, then stir in the yogurt, cream and garam masala. Pour the sauce over the vegetables and garnish with fresh coriander. Serve with poppadums.

Variation
Any combination of vegetables can be used for this korma, including carrots, cauliflower, broccoli, peas and chickpeas.

Tofu & Green Bean Red Curry

This Thai curry is simple and quick to make.

Serves 4–6
600ml/1 pint/2½ cups
 coconut milk
15ml/1 tbsp red curry paste
45ml/3 tbsp vegetarian "oyster"
 sauce (mushroom-based)
10ml/2 tsp sugar
225g/8oz/3¼ cups button
 (white) mushrooms
115g/4oz green beans, trimmed
175g/6oz firm tofu, cut into
 2cm/ ¾in cubes
4 kaffir lime leaves, torn
2 fresh red chillies, sliced
fresh coriander (cilantro) leaves,
 to garnish

1 Pour about one-third of the coconut milk into a pan. Cook until it starts to separate and an oily sheen appears.

2 Stir in the curry paste, "oyster" sauce and sugar, then add the mushrooms. Stir and cook for 1 minute. Stir in the rest of the coconut milk and bring to the boil. Add the beans and tofu and simmer gently for 4–5 minutes more. Stir in the lime leaves and chillies. Serve immediately, garnished with the coriander leaves.

Tofu with Chillies

This is quick, easy and deliciously spicy.

Serves 4
450g/1lb tofu, diced
15ml/1tbsp dark soy sauce
4 fresh red Thai chillies
3 garlic cloves
30ml/2 tbsp vegetable oil
30ml/2 tbsp light soy sauce
30ml/2 tbsp vegetarian "oyster"
 sauce (mushroom-based)
15ml/1 tbsp sugar
fresh Thai basil leaves, to garnish

1 Mix the tofu and dark soy sauce in a bowl and set aside to marinate for 10 minutes.
2 Meanwhile, pound the chillies and garlic together to a paste. Heat the oil in a wok and stir-fry the spice paste and tofu for 1 minute. Stir in the remaining ingredients and stir-fry for a further 2 minutes. Serve, garnished with the basil leaves.

Spaghetti with Garlic & Oil

This classic Italian dish has only a few ingredients, which must be of the very best quality. Chilli is always included to give the dish some bite.

Serves 4
400g/14oz fresh or
 dried spaghetti
90ml/6 tbsp extra virgin olive oil
2–4 garlic cloves, chopped
1 dried red chilli
1 small handful of fresh flat leaf
 parsley, coarsely chopped
salt

1 Bring a large pan of generously salted water to the boil and cook the spaghetti until it is *al dente*. Dried spaghetti will take 10–12 minutes; fresh spaghetti will be ready in 2–3 minutes.

2 While the pasta is cooking, heat the oil in a small frying pan over a very low heat. Add the chopped garlic and whole dried chilli and stir over a low heat until the garlic is just beginning to brown. Remove the chilli and save as a garnish.

3 Drain the pasta and tip it into a warmed serving bowl. Pour on the oil and garlic mixture, add the parsley and toss until the pasta glistens. Serve immediately, garnished with the chilli.

Cook's Tips
• *Don't use salt in the oil and garlic mixture, because it will not dissolve sufficiently. This is why plenty of salt is recommended for cooking the pasta.*
• *For an authentic Italian flavour, use* peperoncino, *fiery, dried, red chillies from Abruzzi. They are so hot that they are known locally as* diavoletto – *little devils. They are available from some Italian delicatessens.*

Variation *If you like, serve the pasta with 60ml/4 tbsp freshly grated Parmesan or Pecorino cheese.*

Eliche with Pesto

Bottled pesto is a useful standby, but nothing beats the flavour of the freshly made mixture.

Serves 4
50g/2oz/1½ cups fresh basil
 leaves, plus extra to garnish
2–4 garlic cloves
60ml/4 tbsp pine nuts
120ml/4fl oz/½ cup extra virgin
 olive oil
115g/4oz/1⅓ cups freshly grated
 Parmesan cheese, plus extra,
 shaved, to serve
25g/1oz/⅓ cup freshly grated
 Pecorino cheese
400g/14oz/3½ cups dried eliche
 or other pasta shapes
salt and ground black pepper

1 Put the basil leaves, garlic and pine nuts in a food processor. Add 60ml/4 tbsp of the olive oil. Process until the ingredients are finely chopped, then stop the machine, remove the lid and scrape down the sides of the bowl.

2 Switch the machine on again and slowly add the remaining oil in a thin, steady stream through the feeder tube. You may need to stop the machine and scrape down the sides of the bowl once or twice to make sure everything is evenly mixed.

3 Scrape the mixture into a large bowl and beat in the Parmesan and Pecorino with a wooden spoon. Taste and season with salt and pepper if necessary.

4 Bring a large pan of lightly salted water to the boil and cook the pasta for about 12 minutes, until it is *al dente*. Drain it thoroughly, then add it to the bowl of pesto and toss well. Serve immediately, garnished with the fresh basil leaves. Hand shaved Parmesan separately.

Cook's Tip
The pesto can be made up to 2–3 days in advance. To store pesto, transfer it to a bowl and pour a thin film of olive oil over the surface. Cover the bowl tightly with clear film (plastic wrap) and keep it in the refrigerator.

Fusilli with Wild Mushrooms

A very rich dish with an earthy flavour and lots of garlic, this makes an ideal main course, especially if it is followed by a crisp green salad in the French manner.

Serves 4
½ x 275g/10oz jar wild mushrooms in olive oil
25g/1oz/2 tbsp butter
225g/8oz/3¼ cups fresh wild mushrooms, sliced if large
5ml/1 tsp finely chopped fresh thyme
5ml/1 tsp finely chopped fresh marjoram or oregano
1 garlic cloves, crushed
350g/12oz/3 cups fresh or dried fusilli
250ml/8fl oz/1 cup double (heavy) cream
salt and ground black pepper
fresh thyme and marjoram or oregano, to garnish

1 Drain about 15ml/1 tbsp of the oil from the jar of wild mushrooms into a large, heavy frying pan. Slice or chop the bottled mushrooms into bitesize pieces, if they are large.

2 Add the butter to the oil in the pan and place over a low heat until sizzling. Add the bottled and fresh mushrooms, the chopped herbs and the garlic. Season with salt and pepper to taste. Cook over a low heat, stirring occasionally, for about 10 minutes, until the fresh mushrooms are soft and tender.

3 Bring a large pan of lightly salted water to the boil and cook the pasta until it is *al dente*.

4 Meanwhile, increase the heat under the pan of mushrooms to medium and toss the mixture until all the excess liquid has been driven off.

5 Pour in the cream and bring to the boil, stirring constantly, then taste and add more salt and pepper if needed.

6 Drain the pasta and tip it into a warmed serving bowl. Pour the mushroom sauce over the pasta and toss thoroughly to mix. Serve the fusilli immediately, sprinkled with fresh herb leaves to garnish.

Garganelli with Asparagus & Cream

A lovely recipe for late spring, when bunches of fresh young asparagus are on sale everywhere.

Serves 4
1 bunch fresh young asparagus, about 275g/10oz
350g/12oz/3 cups dried garganelli
25g/1oz/2 tbsp butter
250ml/8fl oz/1 cup double (heavy) cream
30ml/2 tbsp dry white wine
115g/4oz/1⅓ cups freshly grated Parmesan cheese
30ml/2 tbsp chopped fresh mixed herbs
salt and ground black pepper

1 With your fingers, snap off and discard the woody ends of the asparagus. Cut off the tips and set them aside. Cut the stalks diagonally into pieces that are about the same length as the garganelli.

2 Bring a large pan of lightly salted water to the boil and blanch the asparagus stalks for 1 minute. Add the tips and blanch for 1 minute more. Transfer to a colander with a slotted spoon. Rinse under cold water, drain again and set aside.

3 Bring the water in the pan back to the boil, add the pasta and cook until it is *al dente*. Meanwhile, mix the butter and cream in a pan, season to taste and bring to the boil. Simmer for a few minutes, until the cream thickens, then add the asparagus, wine and about half the grated Parmesan. Taste for seasoning and leave over a low heat.

4 Drain the cooked pasta and tip it into a warmed bowl. Pour the sauce over, sprinkle with the fresh herbs and toss well. Serve immediately, topped with the remaining grated Parmesan.

Cook's Tip
When buying asparagus, look for thin, unwrinkled stalks, which will be sweet and tender. The buds should be tight and the stalks should be an even colour.

Indian Mee Goreng

This is a truly international dish combining Indian, Chinese and Western ingredients. It is a delicious treat for lunch or supper.

Serves 4–6
450g/1lb fresh yellow egg noodles
60–90ml/4–6 tbsp vegetable oil
150g/5oz firm tofu, cubed
2 eggs
30ml/2 tbsp water
1 onion, sliced
1 garlic clove, crushed
15ml/1 tbsp light soy sauce
30–45ml/2–3 tbsp
   tomato ketchup
15ml/1 tbsp chilli sauce
1 large cooked potato, diced
4 spring onions
   (scallions), shredded
1–2 fresh green or red chillies,
   seeded and thinly sliced
salt and ground black pepper

1 Bring a large pan of water to the boil, add the fresh egg noodles and cook for just 2 minutes or according to the instructions on the packet. Drain the noodles and immediately rinse them under cold water to prevent any further cooking. Drain well again and then set aside.

2 Heat 30ml/2 tbsp of the oil in a large frying pan. Fry the tofu until brown, then lift it out with a slotted spoon and set it aside.

3 Beat the eggs with the water and a little seasoning. Make an omelette by adding it to the oil in the frying pan and cooking it, without stirring, until it sets. Flip over, cook the other side, then slide it out of the pan, roll up and slice thinly.

4 Heat the remaining oil in a wok and stir-fry the onion and garlic for 2–3 minutes. Add the drained noodles, soy sauce, tomato ketchup and chilli sauce. Toss well over a medium heat for 2 minutes, then add the diced potato.

5 Reserve a few spring onions for garnishing, then stir the rest into the noodles. Add the chillies and the tofu and toss lightly until heated through.

6 Stir in the omelette. Pile on a hot platter, garnish with the remaining spring onions and serve immediately.

Crispy Noodles with Mixed Vegetables

Deep-frying noodles gives them a lovely, crunchy texture. They taste great in this colourful stir-fry.

Serves 3–4
115g/4oz dried vermicelli rice
   noodles or cellophane noodles
groundnut (peanut) oil, for
   deep-frying
115g/4oz yard-long beans or
   green beans, cut into
   short lengths
2.5cm/1in piece of fresh root
   ginger, cut into shreds
1 fresh red chilli, sliced
115g/4oz/1²/₃ cups fresh shiitake
   or button (white) mushrooms,
   thickly sliced
2 large carrots, cut into thin strips
2 courgettes (zucchini), cut into
   thin strips
a few Chinese cabbage leaves,
   coarsely shredded
75g/3oz/³/₄ cup beansprouts
4 spring onions
   (scallions), shredded
30ml/2 tbsp light soy sauce
30ml/2 tbsp Chinese rice wine
5ml/1 tsp sugar
30ml/2 tbsp roughly torn fresh
   coriander (cilantro) leaves

1 Break the noodles into 7.5cm/3in lengths. Half-fill a wok with oil and heat it to 180°C/350°F. Deep-fry the raw noodles, in batches, for 1–2 minutes, until puffed and crispy. Drain on kitchen paper. Carefully pour off all but 30ml/2 tbsp of the oil.

2 Reheat the oil in the wok. When hot, add the beans and stir-fry for 2–3 minutes. Add the ginger, chilli, mushrooms, carrots and courgettes and stir-fry for 1–2 minutes.

3 Add the Chinese cabbage, beansprouts and spring onions. Toss over the heat for 1 minute, then add the soy sauce, rice wine and sugar. Cook, stirring, for about 30 seconds. Add the noodles and coriander and toss gently to mix, without crushing the noodles. Serve immediately, piled on a plate.

Cook's Tip
If a milder flavour is preferred, remove the seeds from the chilli.

Vedgeree with Green Beans & Mushrooms

Crunchy green beans and mushrooms are the star ingredients in this vegetarian version of an old favourite.

Serves 2
115g/4oz/³⁄₄ cup basmati rice
3 eggs
175g/6oz/1½ cups green
    beans, trimmed
50g/2oz/¼ cup butter
1 onion, finely chopped
225g/8oz/3¼ cups brown cap
    (cremini) mushrooms, quartered
30ml/2 tbsp single
    (light) cream
15ml/1 tbsp chopped
    fresh parsley
salt and ground black pepper

1 Rinse the rice several times in cold water. Drain thoroughly. Bring a large pan of lightly salted water to the boil, add the rice and cook for 10–12 minutes, until tender. Drain thoroughly and set aside.

2 Half fill a second pan with water, add the eggs and bring to the boil over a medium heat. Lower the heat and simmer gently for 8 minutes. Drain the eggs, cool them under cold water, then remove the shells.

3 Bring another pan of water to the boil and cook the green beans for 5 minutes. Drain, refresh under cold running water, then drain again.

4 Melt the butter in a large, heavy frying pan. Add the onion and mushrooms and cook over a moderate heat, stirring occasionally, for 2–3 minutes.

5 Stir in the beans and rice and cook for 2 minutes. Cut the hard-boiled eggs into wedges and add them to the pan.

6 Stir in the cream and parsley, taking care not to break up the eggs. Season to taste with salt and pepper. Reheat the vedgeree, but do not allow it to boil. Transfer to a warmed serving dish and serve immediately.

Golden Vegetable Paella

Hearty enough for the hungriest guests, this takes very little time to prepare and cook.

Serves 4
pinch of saffron threads
750ml/1¼ pints/3 cups hot
    Vegetable Stock
90ml/6 tbsp olive oil
2 large onions, sliced
3 garlic cloves, chopped
275g/10oz/1½ cups long
    grain rice
50g/2oz/⅓ cup wild rice
175g/6oz pumpkin, chopped
1 large carrot, cut into
    thin batons
1 yellow (bell) pepper, seeded
    and sliced
4 tomatoes, peeled and chopped
115g/4oz/1²⁄₃ cups oyster
    mushrooms, quartered
salt and ground black pepper
strips of red, yellow and green
    (bell) pepper, to garnish

1 Place the saffron in a small bowl with 60ml/4 tbsp of the hot stock. Leave to stand for 5 minutes.

2 Meanwhile, heat the oil in a paella pan or large, heavy frying pan. Add the onions and garlic and cook over a low heat, stirring occasionally, for 3 minutes, until just beginning to soften.

3 Add the long grain rice and wild rice to the pan and toss for 2–3 minutes, until coated in oil. Add the stock to the pan, together with the pumpkin and the saffron threads and liquid. Stir the mixture as it comes to the boil, then reduce the heat to the lowest setting.

4 Cover and cook very gently for 15 minutes, without lifting the lid. Add the carrot batons, yellow pepper and chopped tomatoes and season to taste with salt and pepper. Replace the lid and cook very gently for a further 5 minutes, or until the rice is almost tender.

5 Add the oyster mushrooms, check the seasoning and cook, uncovered, for just enough time to soften the mushrooms without letting the paella stick to the pan. Garnish with the peppers and serve immediately.

Chinese Fried Rice

This is a great way to use leftover cooked rice. It not only looks colourful, but also tastes delicious.

Serves 4–6

60ml/4 tbsp oil
115g/4oz shallots, halved and
   thinly sliced
3 garlic cloves, crushed
1 fresh red chilli, seeded and
   finely chopped
6 spring onions (scallions),
   finely chopped
1 red (bell) pepper, seeded and
   finely chopped
225g/8oz white cabbage,
   finely shredded
175g/6oz cucumber,
   finely chopped
50g/2oz/ ½ cup frozen
   peas, thawed
3 eggs, beaten
5ml/1 tsp tomato purée (paste)
30ml/2 tbsp freshly squeezed
   lime juice
1.5ml/ ¼ tsp Tabasco sauce
675g/1½lb/6 cups very cold
   cooked white rice
115g/4oz/1 cup cashew nuts,
   coarsely chopped
about 30ml/2 tbsp chopped
   fresh coriander (cilantro), plus
   extra to garnish
salt and ground black pepper

1 Heat the oil in a wok. Add the shallots and cook, stirring frequently, until very crisp and golden. Remove with a slotted spoon and drain well on kitchen paper.

2 Add the garlic and chilli and cook for 1 minute. Add the spring onions and red pepper and cook for 3–4 minutes, or until beginning to soften. Add the cabbage, cucumber and peas and cook for 2 minutes more.

3 Make a gap and add the beaten eggs. Scramble the eggs, stirring occasionally, then stir them into the vegetables.

4 Stir in the tomato purée, lime juice and Tabasco. Add the rice, cashews and coriander, with plenty of seasoning. Toss over a high heat for 3–4 minutes, until the rice is piping hot. Serve garnished with the crisp shallots and coriander.

Egyptian Rice with Lentils

Two important staple foods come together in this simple, but tasty Middle-Eastern dish, which owes its warm flavour to the inclusion of ground cumin and cinnamon. Note that, although split red lentils are also known as Egyptian lentils, they are not suitable for this dish.

Serves 6

350g/12oz/1½ cups large
   brown lentils
2 large onions
45ml/3 tbsp olive oil
15ml/1 tbsp ground cumin
2.5ml/ ½ tsp ground cinnamon
225g/8oz/generous 1 cup long
   grain rice
salt and ground black pepper
flat leaf parsley, to garnish

1 Put the lentils in a large pan. Add enough water to cover them by 5cm/2in. Bring to the boil, lower the heat, cover and simmer for 30–45 minutes, or until tender. Drain thoroughly.

2 Finely chop one onion, and slice the other. Heat 15ml/1 tbsp of the oil in a pan. Add the chopped onion and cook over a low heat, stirring occasionally, for 5 minutes, until soft. Add the lentils, cumin and cinnamon. Stir well and season to taste with salt and pepper.

3 Measure the volume of rice and add it, with the same volume of water, to the lentil mixture. Cover and simmer for about 20 minutes, until both the rice and lentils are tender.

4 Meanwhile, heat the remaining oil in a frying pan and cook the sliced onion for about 15 minutes, until very dark brown.

5 Tip the rice mixture into a serving bowl, sprinkle with the sliced onion and serve immediately, garnished with flat leaf parsley. Alternatively, leave to cool before serving.

Cook's Tip
Use two 400g/14oz cans of cooked lentils, if you like. Simply add them to the cooked chopped onion in Step 2.

Goat's Cheese Kasha

Kasha is a Russian staple of cooked grains. Buckwheat is conventionally used, but has a strong flavour. Here it is moderated with couscous.

Serves 4

175g/6oz/1 cup couscous
45ml/3 tbsp buckwheat
15g/½oz/¼ cup dried ceps
3 eggs, lightly beaten
60ml/4 tbsp chopped
   fresh parsley

10ml/2 tsp chopped fresh thyme
60ml/4 tbsp olive oil
45ml/3 tbsp walnut oil
175g/6oz crumbly white
   goat's cheese
50g/2oz/½ cup broken
   walnuts, toasted
salt and ground black pepper
fresh parsley sprigs,
   to garnish
rye bread and a mixed salad,
   to serve

1 Place the couscous, buckwheat and ceps in a bowl, cover with boiling water and leave to soak for 15 minutes. Drain off any excess liquid.

2 Place the mixture in a large non-stick frying pan and stir in the eggs. Season with plenty of salt and pepper. Cook over a medium heat, stirring with a wooden spoon until the mixture looks like grainy scrambled eggs. Do not let it get too dry.

3 Stir in the parsley, thyme, olive oil and walnut oil. Crumble in the goat's cheese and stir in the walnuts.

4 Transfer to a large serving dish, garnish with fresh parsley sprigs, and serve hot with rye bread and a mixed salad.

Cook's Tip
Cep is the popular name for the Boletus edulis mushroom. It is also known as the penny bun in England. As the dried mushrooms are widely used in Italian cuisine, packets may also be labelled porcini (little pigs), the Italian name. Dried bay boletus mushrooms (Boletus badius) are also available, but the flavour is inferior to that of ceps.

Aubergine Pilaff

This hearty dish is made with bulgur wheat and aubergine, flavoured with fresh mint, for a deliciously unusual touch.

Serves 2

2 medium aubergines (eggplant)
60–90ml/4–6 tbsp sunflower oil
1 small onion, finely chopped
175g/6oz/1 cup bulgur wheat

450ml/¾ pint/scant 2 cups
   Vegetable Stock
30ml/2 tbsp pine nuts, toasted
15ml/1 tbsp chopped fresh mint
salt and ground black pepper

For the garnish
lime wedges
lemon wedges
torn fresh mint leaves

1 Trim the ends from the aubergines, then slice them lengthways. Cut each slice into neat sticks and then into 1cm/½in dice.

2 Heat 60ml/4 tbsp of the oil in a large, heavy frying pan. Add the onion and cook over a medium heat for 1 minute. Add the diced aubergine. Increase the heat to high and cook, stirring frequently, for about 4 minutes, until just tender. Add the remaining oil if needed.

3 Stir in the bulgur wheat, mixing well, then pour in the vegetable stock. Bring to the boil, then lower the heat and simmer for 10 minutes, or until all the liquid has evaporated. Season to taste with salt and pepper.

4 Stir in the pine nuts and mint, then spoon the pilaff on to individual plates. Garnish each portion with lime and lemon wedges. Sprinkle with torn mint leaves for extra colour and serve immediately.

Variation
Use courgettes (zucchini) instead of aubergine (eggplant), or, for something completely different, substitute acorn squash.

MIDWEEK MEALS

We all have a repertoire of standard dishes and family favourites, but it is all too easy to get stuck in a rut when preparing midweek suppers. Time is short for planning, shopping and cooking and the last thing anyone feels like is experimenting with new dishes that might take forever to prepare and the family might not even like. This chapter offers clever twists on familiar favourites, as well as some exciting new ideas. If everyone's enthusiasm for cauliflower cheese seems to have drained away, maybe Gorgonzola, Cauliflower & Walnut Gratin will arouse their interest.

If you have never made your own burgers, try one of the two recipes in this chapter and you will never buy a pack from a supermarket again – apart from anything else, your family wouldn't let you.

There are lots of good ideas based on a wide range of ingredients, from rice and other grains to root and green vegetables and from tofu to cheese. Filling stews and baked dishes are perfect winter warmers, while lighter vegetable medleys are easy to cook and even easier to eat on summer evenings. Home-made pizza can be eaten at any time of year and, in some families, at any time of day, while stir-fries are so versatile they can be easily adapted to suit everyone's taste. Use the recipes here to turn cooking midweek meals from a chore into a pleasure.

Vegetable Crumble

This dish is perennially popular with children, and even those who claim to dislike Brussels sprouts will tuck into it eagerly.

Serves 8
450g/1lb potatoes, peeled and halved
25g/1oz/2 tbsp butter
225g/8oz leeks, sliced
450g/1lb carrots, chopped
2 garlic cloves, crushed
225g/8oz/3¼ cups mushrooms, thinly sliced
450g/1lb Brussels sprouts, sliced
salt and ground black pepper

For the cheese crumble
50g/2oz/½ cup plain (all-purpose) flour
50g/2oz/¼ cup butter
50g/2oz/1 cup fresh white breadcrumbs
50g/2oz/½ cup grated Cheddar cheese
30ml/2 tbsp chopped fresh parsley
5ml/1 tsp English (hot) mustard powder

1 Add the potatoes to a pan of lightly salted water. Bring them to the boil and cook for about 15 minutes, until just tender.

2 Meanwhile, melt the butter in a large pan. Add the leeks and carrots and cook over a low heat, stirring occasionally, for 2–3 minutes. Add the garlic and mushrooms and cook, stirring occasionally, for 3 minutes more.

3 Add the Brussels sprouts to the pan. Season to taste with pepper. Transfer the vegetable mixture to a 2.5 litre/4 pint/10 cup ovenproof dish.

4 Preheat the oven to 200°C/400°F/Gas 6. Drain the potatoes and cut them into 1cm/½in thick slices. Arrange them in an even layer on top of the other vegetables.

5 To make the crumble, sift the flour into a bowl and rub in the butter with your fingertips. Alternatively, process in a food processor until combined. Add the breadcrumbs and mix in the grated Cheddar, parsley and mustard powder. Spoon the crumble mixture evenly over the vegetables and bake for 20–30 minutes. Serve hot.

Gorgonzola, Cauliflower & Walnut Gratin

A bubbly blue cheese sauce sprinkled with chopped nuts makes a marvellous topping for cauliflower.

Serves 4
1 large cauliflower, broken into florets
25g/1oz/2 tbsp butter
1 medium onion, finely chopped
45ml/3 tbsp plain (all-purpose) flour
450ml/¾ pint/scant 2 cups milk
150g/5oz Gorgonzola cheese, cut into pieces
2.5ml/½ tsp celery salt
pinch of cayenne pepper
75g/3oz/¾ cup chopped walnuts
salt
fresh parsley, to garnish

1 Bring a large pan of lightly salted water to the boil and cook the cauliflower for 6 minutes. Drain and place in a flameproof gratin dish.

2 Heat the butter in a heavy pan. Add the onion and cook over a low heat, stirring occasionally, for 4–5 minutes, until softened but not coloured.

3 Stir in the flour and cook, stirring constantly, for 1 minute, then gradually add the milk, stirring until the sauce boils and thickens. Stir in the cheese, celery salt and cayenne.

4 Preheat the grill (broiler) to moderately hot. Spoon the sauce over the cauliflower, sprinkle with the chopped walnuts and grill (broil) until golden. Garnish with the parsley and serve.

Variations
• For a delicious alternative, replace the cauliflower with 1.1kg/2½lb fresh broccoli or use a combination.
• For a milder flavour, use Dolcelatte or Buxton blue cheese instead of Gorgonzola.
• For an even richer sauce, substitute 250ml/8fl oz/1 cup single (light) cream for the same quantity of milk.

Pan Haggerty

A wonderfully old-fashioned dish, this has endured because it is easy to make and always tastes delicious.

Serves 2
30ml/2 tbsp olive oil
25g/1oz/2 tbsp butter

450g/1lb potatoes, thinly sliced
1 large onion, halved and sliced
2 garlic cloves, crushed
115g/4oz/1 cup grated mature
   (sharp) Cheddar cheese
45ml/3 tbsp chopped fresh
   chives, plus extra to garnish
salt and ground black pepper

1 Heat the oil and butter in a large heavy frying pan which can safely be used under the grill (broiler). (Cover a wooden handle with foil to protect it.) Remove the pan from the heat and cover the base with a layer of potatoes, followed by layers of onion, garlic, cheese, chives and seasoning.

2 Continue layering, ending with cheese. Cover with foil and cook over a gentle heat for about 30 minutes, or until the potatoes and onion are tender. Remove the foil.

3 Preheat the grill and slide the frying pan under it. Cook until the topping has browned. Garnish with chives and serve.

Bubble & Squeak

Another classic British dish, this is very easy to make. It is a traditional way of using up leftover vegetables, but is also worth cooking with fresh ingredients.

Serves 4
500g/1¼lb/6 cups
   mashed potato
225g/8oz/2 cups cooked cabbage
60ml/4 tbsp sunflower oil
salt and ground black pepper

1 Mix together the potato and cabbage and season to taste.
2 Heat the oil in a frying pan. Add the potato mixture and press down to make a cake. Cook over a low heat until golden underneath. Invert on to a plate and return to the pan. Cook for about 10 minutes more, until golden.

Root Vegetable Gratin with Indian Spices

Subtly spiced with curry powder, turmeric, coriander and mild chilli powder, this rich gratin is substantial enough to serve on its own for lunch or supper.

Serves 4
2 large potatoes, total weight
   about 450g/1lb
2 sweet potatoes, total weight
   about 275g/10oz
175g/6oz celeriac

15g/½oz/1 tbsp butter
5ml/1 tsp curry powder
5ml/1 tsp ground turmeric
2.5ml/½ tsp ground coriander
5ml/1 tsp mild chilli powder
3 shallots, chopped
150ml/¼ pint/⅔ cup single
   (light) cream
150ml/¼ pint/⅔ cup semi-
   skimmed (low-fat) milk
salt and ground black pepper
chopped fresh flat leaf parsley,
   to garnish

1 Using a sharp knife or the slicing attachment of a food processor, slice the potatoes, sweet potatoes and celeriac thinly. Immediately place the vegetables in a bowl of cold water to prevent them from discolouring.

2 Preheat the oven to 180°C/350°F/Gas 4. Heat half the butter in a heavy pan, and add the curry powder, turmeric, coriander and half the chilli powder. Cook for 2 minutes, then leave to cool slightly.

3 Drain the vegetables, then pat them dry with kitchen paper. Place them in a bowl, add the spice mixture and the shallots and mix well.

4 Arrange the vegetables in a gratin dish, seasoning each layer. Mix together the cream and milk. Pour the mixture over the vegetables, then sprinkle the remaining chilli powder on top.

5 Cover with greaseproof (waxed) paper and bake for 45 minutes. Remove the greaseproof paper, dot with the remaining butter and bake for 50 minutes more, until the top is golden. Serve garnished with chopped fresh parsley.

Cheese & Leek Sausages with Spicy Tomato Sauce

These are based on Glamorgan sausages, which are traditionally made using white or wholemeal (whole-wheat) breadcrumbs alone. However, adding a little mashed potato lightens the sausages and makes them much easier to handle.

Serves 4
25g/1oz/2 tbsp butter
175g/6oz leeks, finely chopped
90ml/6 tbsp cold mashed potato
115g/4oz/2 cups fresh
    white breadcrumbs
150g/5oz/1¼ cups grated
    Caerphilly cheese
30ml/2 tbsp chopped
    fresh parsley
5ml/1 tsp chopped fresh sage
2 large (US extra large)
    eggs, beaten

cayenne pepper
65g/2½ oz/1 cup dry
    white breadcrumbs
oil, for shallow frying
salt and ground black pepper

For the sauce
30ml/2 tbsp olive oil
2 garlic cloves, thinly sliced
1 fresh red chilli, seeded and
    finely chopped
1 small onion, finely chopped
500g/1¼lb tomatoes, peeled,
    seeded and chopped
2–3 fresh thyme sprigs
10ml/2 tsp balsamic vinegar
pinch of light muscovado
    (molasses) sugar
15–30ml/1–2 tbsp chopped
    fresh marjoram

1 Melt the butter in a frying pan. Add the leeks and cook over a low heat, stirring occasionally, for 4–5 minutes, until softened but not browned.

2 Mix the leeks with the mashed potato, fresh breadcrumbs, cheese, parsley and sage. Add two-thirds of the beaten eggs to bind the mixture. Season with salt and pepper and cayenne.

3 Shape the mixture into 12 sausages. Put the remaining egg in a shallow dish and the dry breadcrumbs in another shallow dish. Dip the sausages first in egg, then in the breadcrumbs. Place the coated sausages on a plate, cover and chill.

4 To make the sauce, heat the olive oil over a low heat. Add the garlic, chilli and onion and cook, stirring occasionally, for 3–4 minutes. Add the tomatoes, thyme and vinegar. Season to taste with salt, pepper and sugar.

5 Cook the sauce for 40–50 minutes, until much reduced. Remove the thyme and process the sauce in a blender to a purée. Return to the clean pan and add the marjoram. Reheat gently, then adjust the seasoning, adding more sugar, if necessary.

6 Fry the sausages in shallow oil until golden brown on all sides. Drain on kitchen paper and serve with the sauce.

> **Variation**
> These sausages are also delicious served with aioli, guacamole or chilli jam.

Mixed Vegetables with Artichokes

Baking a vegetable medley in the oven is a wonderfully easy way of producing a quick, simple, wholesome midweek meal.

Serves 4
30ml/2 tbsp olive oil
675g/1½lb frozen broad
    (fava) beans

4 turnips, peeled and sliced
4 leeks, sliced
1 red (bell) pepper, seeded
    and sliced
200g/7oz fresh spinach leaves
2 x 400g/14oz cans artichoke
    hearts, drained
60ml/4 tbsp pumpkin seeds
soy sauce
salt and ground black pepper

1 Preheat the oven to 180°C/350°F/Gas 4. Pour the olive oil into a casserole and set aside.

2 Cook the broad beans in a pan of lightly salted boiling water for about 10 minutes.

3 Drain the broad beans and place them in the casserole. Add the turnips, leeks, red pepper slices, spinach and canned artichoke hearts.

4 Cover the casserole and place it in the oven. Bake for 30–40 minutes, or until the turnips are soft.

5 Stir in the pumpkin seeds and a little soy sauce to taste. Season with ground black pepper and serve.

> **Cook's Tip**
> Serve this with pasta, rice, new potatoes or bread.

> **Variation**
> For a delicious change, top the cooked vegetables with a mixture of wholemeal (whole-wheat) breadcrumbs and grated Cheddar cheese. Grill (broil) until the cheese melts.

Potato Rösti & Tofu Stacks

Although this dish has several components, it is not difficult to make. Serve it with mixed salad leaves.

Serves 4
425g/15oz firm tofu, cut into
    1cm/½in cubes
4 large potatoes, total weight
    about 900g/2lb, peeled
sunflower oil, for frying
30ml/2 tbsp sesame
    seeds, toasted
salt and ground black pepper

For the marinade
30ml/2 tbsp tamari or dark
    soy sauce
15ml/1 tbsp clear honey
2 garlic cloves, crushed
4cm/1½in piece of fresh root
    ginger, grated
5ml/1 tsp toasted sesame oil

For the sauce
15ml/1 tbsp olive oil
8 tomatoes, halved, seeded
    and chopped

1 Mix all the marinade ingredients in a shallow dish. Add the tofu, spoon the marinade over and marinate for 1 hour.

2 Cook the potatoes in a large pan of boiling water for 10–15 minutes, until almost tender. Leave to cool, then grate coarsely. Season well. Preheat the oven to 200°C/400°F/Gas 6.

3 Lift out the tofu from the marinade. Spread it out on a baking sheet and bake for 20 minutes, turning occasionally, until the cubes are golden and crisp.

4 Form the potato mixture into four cakes. Heat a frying pan with just enough oil to cover the base. Place the cakes in the pan and flatten them to rounds about 1cm/½in thick. Cook for 6 minutes, until golden and crisp underneath. Carefully turn them over and cook the undersides for 6 minutes, until golden.

5 Meanwhile, make the sauce. Heat the oil in a pan, add the reserved marinade and the tomatoes and simmer, stirring occasionally, for 10 minutes. Press through a sieve, then reheat.

6 To serve, place a rösti on each plate. Pile the tofu on top, spoon over the sauce and sprinkle with the sesame seeds.

Tomato Bread & Butter Pudding

This is a great family dish and is ideal when you don't have time to cook on the day, because it can be prepared in advance.

Serves 4
50g/2oz/¼ cup butter, softened
15ml/1 tbsp red pesto sauce
1 garlic and herb focaccia
150g/5oz mozzarella cheese,
    thinly sliced
2 large ripe tomatoes, sliced
300ml/½ pint/1¼ cups milk
3 large (US extra large) eggs
5ml/1 tsp fresh chopped oregano,
    plus extra leaves to garnish
50g/2oz/½ cup grated
    Pecorino cheese
salt and ground black pepper

1 Preheat the oven to 180°C/350°F/Gas 4. Mix the butter and pesto sauce in a small bowl. Slice the herb bread and spread one side of each slice with the pesto mixture.

2 In an oval ovenproof dish, layer the slices of herb bread with the mozzarella and tomatoes, overlapping each new layer with the next.

3 Beat the milk, eggs and oregano in a jug (pitcher), season well with salt and pepper and pour over the bread. Leave to stand for at least 5 minutes.

4 Sprinkle over the grated cheese and bake the pudding for 40 minutes, or until golden brown and just set. Sprinkle with whole oregano leaves and serve immediately.

> **Cook's Tip**
> The longer this stands before baking, the better it will be. Try to leave it for at least half an hour before baking, if you have time.

> **Variation**
> Other cheeses that would go well with this pudding include Fontina, Beaufort, Bel Paese and Taleggio.

Pasta with Slow-cooked Cabbage, Parmesan & Pine Nuts

This is an unusual, but quite delicious, way of serving pasta. Use cavolo nero, Italy's delicious black cabbage, if you can locate it.

Serves 4
25g/1oz/2 tbsp butter
15ml/1 tbsp extra virgin olive oil
500g/1¼lb Spanish onions, halved and thinly sliced
5–10ml/1–2 tsp balsamic vinegar
400g/14oz cavolo nero, spring greens (collards) or kale, shredded
450g/1lb/4 cups dried pasta, such as penne or fusilli
75g/3oz/1 cup freshly grated Parmesan cheese
50g/2oz/½ cup pine nuts, toasted
salt and ground black pepper

1 Heat the butter and olive oil in a large pan. Add the onions, stirring to coat them in the butter mixture. Cover and cook over a very low heat, stirring occasionally, for about 20 minutes, until the onions are very soft.

2 Remove the lid and continue to cook the onions until they have turned golden yellow. Add the balsamic vinegar and season well with salt and pepper, then cook for a further 1–2 minutes. Set aside.

3 Bring a large pan of lightly salted water to the boil and blanch the greens for about 3 minutes. Remove the greens from the pan using a slotted spoon and drain them thoroughly. Add them to the onions, stir thoroughly to mix and cook over the lowest possible heat.

4 Bring the water in the pan back to the boil, add the pasta and cook for about 12 minutes, until *al dente*. Drain and return it to the pan. Add the onion mixture and toss over a medium heat until warmed through.

5 Season well with salt and pepper and stir in half the grated Parmesan. Spoon on to warmed plates. Sprinkle the pine nuts and more Parmesan on top and serve immediately.

Rustic Buckwheat Pasta Bake

A spicy combination of nutty-flavoured buckwheat pasta, vegetables and Fontina cheese, this makes a wonderful family supper.

Serves 6
45ml/3 tbsp olive oil, plus extra for greasing
2 potatoes, peeled and cubed
225g/8oz/2 cups dried buckwheat pasta shapes
275g/10oz/2½ cups shredded Savoy cabbage
1 onion, chopped
2 leeks, sliced
2 garlic cloves, chopped
175g/6oz/2½ cups brown cap (cremini) mushrooms, sliced
5ml/1 tsp caraway seeds
5ml/1 tsp cumin seeds
150ml/¼ pint/⅔ cup Vegetable Stock
150g/5oz Fontina cheese, diced
25g/1oz/¼ cup walnuts, coarsely chopped
salt and ground black pepper

1 Preheat the oven to 200°C/400°F/Gas 6. Grease a deep ovenproof dish with oil. Cook the cubed potatoes in a pan of lightly salted water for 8–10 minutes, until tender, then drain and set aside.

2 Meanwhile, bring a large pan of lightly salted water to the boil. Add the pasta and cook until it is *al dente*. Add the cabbage in the last minute of cooking time. Drain, then rinse under cold running water.

3 Heat the olive oil in a large heavy pan. Add the onion and leeks and cook over a medium heat, stirring occasionally, for 5 minutes, until softened.

4 Add the garlic and mushrooms and cook, stirring occasionally, for 3 minutes more, until tender. Stir in the caraway seeds and cumin seeds and cook, stirring constantly, for 1 minute.

5 Stir in the cooked potatoes, pasta and cabbage. Season well with salt and pepper. Spoon the mixture into the prepared dish. Pour the stock over the mixture, then sprinkle with the diced cheese and walnuts. Bake for 15 minutes, or until the cheese is melted and bubbling.

Stir-fried Tofu & Beansprouts

Tofu is a boon to the busy vegetarian cook, providing plenty of protein in this simple stir-fry.

Serves 4
225g/8oz firm tofu
groundnut (peanut) oil, for
    deep-frying
175g/6oz medium egg noodles
15ml/1 tbsp sesame oil
5ml/1 tsp cornflour (cornstarch)
10ml/2 tsp dark soy sauce

30ml/1 tbsp Chinese rice wine
5ml/1 tsp sugar
6–8 spring onions (scallions), cut
    diagonally into 2.5cm/
    1in lengths
3 garlic cloves, sliced
1 fresh green chilli, seeded
    and sliced
115g/4oz pak choi (bok choy)
    leaves, coarsely shredded
50g/2oz/1 cup beansprouts
50g/2oz/½ cup cashew
    nuts, toasted

1 Drain the tofu and pat it dry with kitchen paper. Cut it into 2.5cm/1in cubes. Half fill a wok with oil and heat to 180°C/350°F or until a cube of day-old bread browns in 30 seconds. Deep-fry the tofu, in batches, for 1–2 minutes, until golden. Remove with a slotted spoon and drain on kitchen paper. Carefully pour all but 30ml/2 tbsp of the oil from the wok.

2 Bring a large pan of water to the boil, add the noodles and remove the pan from the heat. Cover and leave to stand for about 4 minutes, until the noodles are just tender. Drain, rinse under cold water and drain again. Toss in 10ml/2 tsp of the sesame oil and set aside.

3 In a bowl, blend together the cornflour, soy sauce, rice wine, sugar and the remaining sesame oil.

4 Reheat the 30ml/2 tbsp of groundnut oil in the wok. Add the spring onions, garlic, chilli, pak choi and beansprouts and stir-fry for 1–2 minutes.

5 Add the tofu cubes, together with the noodles and sauce. Cook, stirring, for about 1 minute, until thoroughly mixed and heated through. Transfer to a warmed serving dish, sprinkle over the cashew nuts and serve immediately.

Peanut Noodles

Add any of your favourite vegetables to this quick and easy recipe and increase the number of chillies, if you can take the heat!

Serves 4
200g/7oz medium egg noodles
30ml/2 tbsp olive oil
2 garlic cloves, crushed
1 large onion, coarsely chopped
1 red (bell) pepper, seeded and
    coarsely chopped
1 yellow (bell) pepper, seeded and
    coarsely chopped
350g/12oz courgettes (zucchini),
    coarsely chopped

150g/5oz/1¼ cups roasted
    unsalted peanuts,
    coarsely chopped
chopped fresh chives, to garnish

For the dressing
60ml/4 tbsp olive oil
grated rind and juice of 1 lemon
1 fresh red chilli, seeded and
    finely chopped
45ml/3 tbsp chopped fresh chives
15–30ml/1–2 tbsp
    balsamic vinegar
salt and ground black pepper

1 Bring a large pan of water to the boil, add the noodles and remove the pan from the heat. Cover and leave to stand for about 4 minutes, until the noodles are tender. Drain, rinse under cold water and drain again.

2 Heat the olive oil in a wok. Add the garlic and onion and stir-fry for 3–4 minutes, until the onion is beginning to soften. Add the red and yellow peppers and the courgettes and stir-fry for 3–4 minutes, until crisp-tender. Add the peanuts and cook for 1 minute more.

3 Make the dressing. In a jug (pitcher), whisk together the olive oil, grated lemon rind and 45ml/3 tbsp of the lemon juice. Add the chilli and chives and whisk in balsamic vinegar to taste. Season well with salt and pepper.

4 Add the noodles to the vegetables and toss briefly over the heat. Add the dressing and stir to coat. Transfer to a warmed serving dish and serve immediately, garnished with chives.

Fiorentina Pizza

An egg adds the finishing touch to this spinach pizza; it's best when the yolk is still slightly soft.

Serves 2–3
45ml/3 tbsp olive oil
1 small red onion, thinly sliced
175g/6oz fresh spinach,
   stalks removed
1 pizza base, about
   25–30cm/10–12in in diameter
350ml/12fl oz/1½ cups
   Tomato Sauce
freshly grated nutmeg
150g/5oz mozzarella cheese
1 egg
25g/1oz/¼ cup grated
   Gruyère cheese

1 Heat 15ml/1 tbsp of the olive oil. Add the onion and cook over a low heat, stirring occasionally, for 5 minutes, until soft. Add the spinach and cook until wilted. Drain any excess liquid.

2 Preheat the oven to 220°C/425°F/Gas 7. Support the pizza base on a baking sheet, then brush it with half the remaining olive oil. Spread the tomato sauce evenly over the base, using the back of a spoon, leaving a 1cm/½in rim all around. Then cover the top of the pizza with the spinach mixture. Sprinkle over a little freshly grated nutmeg.

3 Slice the mozzarella thinly and arrange it over the spinach. Drizzle over the remaining oil. Bake for 10 minutes, then remove from the oven.

4 Make a small well in the centre of the pizza topping and carefully break the egg into the hole. Sprinkle over the grated Gruyère. Return the pizza to the oven for 5–10 minutes, until crisp and golden. Serve immediately.

> **Variation**
> If you make your own dough, you can easily transform this into a calzone. Add the egg to the spinach mixture, spread it over half the pizza base, then add the cheeses. Fold the pizza base over, seal the edges and bake for 20 minutes.

Butternut Squash & Sage Pizza

The combination of the sweet butternut squash, pungent sage and sharp goat's cheese works wonderfully on this pizza.

Serves 2–3
15g/½oz/1 tbsp butter
30ml/2 tbsp olive oil
1 shallot, finely chopped
1 small butternut squash, peeled,
   seeded and cubed
8 fresh sage leaves
1 pizza base, about
   25–30cm/10–12in in diameter
350ml/12fl oz/1½ cups
   Tomato Sauce
75g/3oz mozzarella cheese, sliced
75g/3oz firm goat's cheese
salt and ground black pepper

1 Preheat the oven to 200°C/400°F/Gas 6. Melt the butter in the oil in a roasting pan. Add the shallot, squash and half the sage leaves. Toss well to coat all over in the oil mixture. Roast the vegetables for 15–20 minutes, until tender.

2 Increase the oven temperature to 220°C/425°F/Gas 7. Support the pizza base on a baking sheet. Spread the tomato sauce evenly over the surface with the back of a spoon, leaving a 1cm/½in rim all around.

3 Spoon the squash and shallot mixture evenly over the pizza, arrange the slices of mozzarella on top and crumble the goat's cheese over the surface.

4 Sprinkle the remaining sage leaves over the pizza and season with plenty of salt and pepper. Bake for 15–20 minutes, until the cheese has melted and the crust is golden. Serve immediately.

> **Cook's Tip**
> If you don't have time to make a yeast-based pizza dough, use a scone mixture. Mix 225g/8oz/2 cups self-raising (self-rising) flour with a pinch of salt, then rub in 50g/2oz/¼ cup diced butter. Pour in about 150ml/¼ pint/⅔ cup milk and mix to a soft dough. Pat out to a 25cm/10in round, top as suggested above and bake for about 20 minutes.

Baked Cheese Polenta with Tomato Sauce

Polenta, or cornmeal, is a staple food in Italy. It is boiled in water, and can be eaten soft. This version uses squares of set polenta, baked in a rich tomato sauce.

Serves 4

1 litre/1¾ pints/4 cups water
5ml/1 tsp salt
250g/9oz/2 cups quick-cook polenta
5ml/1 tsp paprika
2.5ml/½ tsp ground nutmeg
30ml/2 tbsp olive oil, plus extra for greasing
1 large onion, finely chopped
2 garlic cloves, crushed
2 x 400g/14oz cans chopped tomatoes
15ml/1 tbsp tomato purée (paste)
5ml/1 tsp sugar
75g/3oz/¾ cup grated Gruyère cheese
salt and ground black pepper

1 Preheat the oven to 200°C/400°F/Gas 6. Line a 28 x 18cm/ 11 x 7in baking tin (pan) with clear film (plastic wrap). Pour the water into a large, heavy pan and add the salt.

2 Bring the water to the boil. Pour in the polenta in a steady stream and cook, stirring constantly, for 5 minutes. Beat in the paprika and nutmeg, then pour the mixture into the prepared tin. Level the surface. Leave to cool.

3 Heat the oil in a pan. Add the onion and garlic and cook over a low heat, stirring occasionally, for 5 minutes, until soft. Stir in the tomatoes, tomato purée and sugar and season with salt and pepper to taste. Simmer for 20 minutes.

4 Turn out the polenta on to a chopping board and cut it into 5cm/2in squares. Place half the polenta squares in a greased ovenproof dish. Spoon over half the tomato sauce and sprinkle with half the grated cheese. Repeat the layers.

5 Bake the polenta for about 25 minutes, until the top is golden and bubbling. Serve immediately.

Polenta with Mushroom Sauce

This is a fine example of just how absolutely delicious soft polenta can be. Topped with a robust mushroom and tomato sauce, it tastes quite sublime.

Serves 4

1.2 litres/2 pints/5 cups Vegetable Stock
350g/12oz/3 cups fine polenta or cornmeal
50g/2oz/⅔ cup freshly grated Parmesan cheese
salt and ground black pepper

For the sauce
15g/½oz/¼ cup dried porcini mushrooms
150ml/¼ pint/⅔ cup hot water
15ml/1 tbsp olive oil
50g/2oz/¼ cup butter
1 onion, finely chopped
1 carrot, finely chopped
1 celery stick, finely chopped
2 garlic cloves, crushed
450g/1lb/6½ cups mixed chestnut and large flat mushrooms, coarsely chopped
120ml/4fl oz/½ cup red wine
400g/14oz can chopped tomatoes
5ml/1 tsp tomato purée (paste)
15ml/1 tbsp chopped fresh thyme

1 Make the sauce. Soak the dried mushrooms in the hot water for 20 minutes. Drain, reserving the liquid, and chop coarsely.

2 Heat the oil and butter in a pan and cook the onion, carrot, celery and garlic for 5 minutes, until beginning to soften. Raise the heat and add both the mushrooms. Cook for another 10 minutes. Pour in the wine and cook rapidly for 2–3 minutes, then add the tomatoes and strained, reserved soaking liquid. Stir in the tomato purée and thyme and season with salt and pepper. Lower the heat and simmer for 20 minutes.

3 Meanwhile, heat the stock in a large heavy pan. Add a pinch of salt. As soon as it simmers, tip in the polenta in a fine stream, whisking until the mixture is smooth. Cook for 30 minutes, stirring constantly, until the polenta comes away from the pan. Stir in half the Parmesan and some pepper.

4 Divide among four heated bowls and top each with sauce. Sprinkle with the remaining Parmesan.

Polenta Pan-pizza

This yeast-free pizza is cooked in a frying pan.

Serves 2
30ml/2 tbsp olive oil
1 large red onion, sliced
3 garlic cloves, crushed
115g/4oz/1⅔ cups brown cap
  (cremini) mushrooms, sliced
5ml/1 tsp dried oregano
115g/4oz mozzarella
  cheese, sliced
tomato wedges and fresh basil
  leaves, to garnish

For the pizza base
50g/2oz/ ½ cup plain (all-
  purpose) flour, sifted
2.5ml/ ½ tsp salt
115g/4oz/scant 1 cup
  fine polenta
5ml/1 tsp baking powder
1 egg, beaten
150ml/ ¼ pint/ ⅔ cup milk
25g/1oz/ ⅓ cup freshly grated
  Parmesan cheese
2.5ml/ ½ tsp dried chilli flakes
15ml/1 tbsp olive oil

1 Heat half the oil in a heavy frying pan and cook the onion for 10 minutes, stirring occasionally. Remove the onion from the pan and set aside Heat the remaining oil in the pan and cook the garlic for 1 minute. Add the mushrooms and oregano and cook for 5 minutes.

2 To make the pizza base, mix the flour, salt, polenta and baking powder in a bowl. Make a well in the centre and add the egg. Gradually add the milk, mixing well to make into a thick, smooth batter. Stir in the Parmesan and chilli flakes.

3 Heat the oil in a 25cm/10in heavy frying pan that can safely be used under the grill (broiler). (Cover a wooden handle with foil to protect it.) Spoon in the batter in an even layer. Cook for 3 minutes, or until set. Remove the pan from the heat and run a knife around the edge of the pizza base. Place a plate over the pan and, holding them together, invert the pizza on to the plate. Slide it back into the pan. Cook for 2 minutes until golden.

4 Preheat the grill to high. Spoon the onion over the pizza base, top with the mushroom mixture and the mozzarella, then grill (broil) for about 6 minutes. Serve in wedges with tomato wedges and basil.

Potato Gnocchi

These tasty Italian dumplings are made with mashed potato and flour.

Serves 4–6
1kg/2¼lb waxy potatoes
250–300g/9–11oz/2¼–2¾ cups
  plain (all-purpose) flour, plus
  more if necessary

1 egg
pinch of freshly grated nutmeg
25g/1oz/2 tbsp butter
salt
fresh basil leaves, shaved
  Parmesan cheese and ground
  black pepper, to garnish

1 Bring a large pan of lightly salted water to the boil. Add the potatoes and cook for 25–30 minutes, until tender, but not falling apart. Drain and peel while the potatoes are still hot.

2 Spread a layer of flour on a work surface. Pass the hot potatoes through a food mill, dropping them directly on to the flour. Sprinkle with about half the remaining flour and mix in very lightly. Break the egg into the mixture. Finally, add the nutmeg to the dough and knead lightly, adding more flour if needed in order to make a dough that is light to the touch and no longer moist.

3 Divide the dough into four pieces. On a lightly floured surface, form each into a roll about 2cm/¾in in diameter. Cut the rolls crossways into pieces about 2cm/¾in long.

4 Press and roll the gnocchi lightly along the tines of a fork towards the points, making ridges on one side, and a depression from your thumb on the other.

5 Bring a large pan of salted water to a fast boil, then drop in about half the prepared gnocchi. As soon as they rise to the surface, after 3–4 minutes, lift them out with a slotted spoon, drain well, and place in a warmed serving bowl. Dot with butter. Cover to keep warm while cooking the remainder.

6 As soon as all the gnocchi are cooked, toss them with the butter, garnish with basil, Parmesan and black pepper and serve.

Kitchiri

This is the Indian original that inspired the classic breakfast dish, kedgeree. Made with basmati rice and small tasty lentils, this will make an ample supper or brunch dish.

Serves 4

115g/4oz/²⁄₃ cup Indian masoor
  dhal or continental green lentils
50g/2oz/¹⁄₄ cup ghee or butter
30ml/2 tbsp sunflower oil
1 onion, chopped
1 garlic clove, crushed
225g/8oz/generous 1 cup easy-
  cook basmati rice
10ml/2 tsp ground coriander
10ml/2 tsp cumin seeds
2 cloves
3 cardamom pods
2 bay leaves
1 cinnamon stick
1 litre/1³⁄₄ pints/4 cups
  Vegetable Stock
30ml/2 tbsp tomato
  purée (paste)
45ml/3 tbsp chopped fresh
  coriander (cilantro) or parsley
salt and ground black pepper

1 Put the dhal or lentils in a bowl. Pour over boiling water to cover and leave to soak for 30 minutes. Meanwhile, bring a pan of water to the boil. Drain the soaked dhal or lentils and add to the pan. Cook for 10 minutes. Drain once more and set aside.

2 Heat the ghee or butter and oil in a large pan and cook the onion and garlic for about 5 minutes.

3 Add the rice, stir well to coat the grains, then stir in the spices. Cook gently for 1–2 minutes, then add the dhal or lentils, stock, tomato purée and seasoning.

4 Bring to the boil, lower the heat, cover and simmer for 20 minutes, until the stock has been absorbed. Stir in the coriander or parsley and check the seasoning. Remove and discard the cinnamon stick and bay leaf and serve.

> **Cook's Tip**
> It is worth growing coriander (cilantro) in a pot, as it has an inimitable flavour and adds authenticity to many ethnic dishes.

Parsnip & Aubergine Biryani

It always seems such a humble vegetable, yet the parsnip has a superb flavour and brings a touch of sweetness to spicy dishes such as this one.

Serves 4–6

1 small aubergine
  (eggplant), sliced
275g/10oz/1¹⁄₄ cups basmati rice
3 onions
2 garlic cloves, coarsely chopped
2.5cm/1in piece of fresh root
  ginger, peeled
45ml/3 tbsp water
about 60ml/4 tbsp vegetable oil
175g/6oz/1¹⁄₂ cups unsalted
  cashew nuts
40g/1¹⁄₂oz/¹⁄₄ cup sultanas
  (golden raisins)
1 red (bell) pepper, seeded
  and sliced
3 parsnips, chopped
5ml/1 tsp ground cumin
5ml/1 tsp ground coriander
2.5ml/¹⁄₂ tsp mild chilli powder
120ml/4fl oz/¹⁄₂ cup natural
  (plain) yogurt
300ml/¹⁄₂ pint/1¹⁄₄ cups
  Vegetable Stock
25g/1oz/2 tbsp butter
salt
fresh coriander (cilantro) sprigs
  and wedges of hard-boiled egg,
  to garnish

1 Layer the aubergine slices in a colander and sprinkle with salt. Leave to drain for 30 minutes. Rinse, pat dry and chop.

2 Soak the rice in cold water while you cook the vegetables. Chop one onion and put it in a food processor or blender with the garlic and ginger. Add the water and process to a paste.

3 Thinly slice the remaining onions. Heat 45ml/3 tbsp of the oil in a large flameproof casserole. Add the onion slices and cook over a low heat, stirring occasionally, for about 10 minutes, until deep golden brown. Remove and drain. Add one-quarter of the cashews to the pan and stir-fry for 2 minutes. Add the sultanas and cook until they swell. Remove and drain.

4 Add the aubergine and red pepper to the casserole and stir-fry for 4–5 minutes. Drain on kitchen paper. Add the parsnips to the casserole and cook for 4–5 minutes. Stir in the remaining cashews and fry for 1 minute. Transfer to a plate with the aubergine and pepper.

5 Add the remaining oil to the casserole. Add the onion paste. Cook, stirring constantly, for 4–5 minutes. Stir in the cumin, ground coriander and chilli powder. Cook, stirring, for 1 minute, then lower the heat and add the yogurt. Stir in the stock, parsnips, aubergine and peppers. Bring to the boil, then lower the heat, cover and simmer for 30–40 minutes, until the parsnips are tender.

6 Preheat the oven to 150°C/300°F/Gas 2. Drain the rice and cook it in salted boiling water for 6 minutes. Drain, then pile in a mound on top of the spiced vegetables. Make a hole from the top to the base using the handle of a wooden spoon.

7 Sprinkle the reserved fried onions, cashew nuts and sultanas over the rice and dot with the butter. Cover with a foil lid. Bake for 35–40 minutes, then spoon on to a warmed serving dish and garnish with the coriander sprigs and egg.

Vegetable Hot-pot with Cheese Triangles

A sort of savoury cobbler, this hot-pot is topped with a scone mixture. The combination is irresistible.

Serves 6
30ml/2 tbsp oil
2 garlic cloves, crushed
1 onion, coarsely chopped
5ml/1 tsp mild chilli powder
450g/1lb potatoes, peeled and coarsely chopped
450g/1lb celeriac, peeled and coarsely chopped
350g/12oz carrots, coarsely chopped
350g/12oz trimmed leeks, coarsely chopped
225g/8oz/3¼ cups brown cap (cremini) mushrooms, halved
20ml/4 tsp plain (all-purpose) flour

600ml/1 pint/2½ cups Vegetable Stock
400g/14oz can chopped tomatoes
15ml/1 tbsp tomato purée (paste)
30ml/2 tbsp chopped fresh thyme
400g/14oz can kidney beans, drained and rinsed
salt and ground black pepper

For the topping
225g/8oz/2 cups self-raising (self-rising) flour
115g/4oz/½ cup butter
115g/4oz/1 cup grated Cheddar cheese
30ml/2 tbsp chopped fresh chives
about 75ml/5 tbsp milk

1 Preheat the oven to 180°C/350°F/Gas 4. Heat the oil in a large flameproof casserole. Add the garlic and onion and cook over a low heat, stirring occasionally, for 5 minutes. Stir in the chilli powder and cook for 1 minute more.

2 Add the potatoes, celeriac, carrots, leeks and mushrooms. Cook for 3–4 minutes. Stir in the flour and cook, stirring constantly, for 1 minute more.

3 Stir in the stock, then the tomatoes, tomato purée and thyme and season well with salt and pepper. Bring to the boil, stirring. Cover and cook in the oven for 30 minutes.

4 Meanwhile, make the topping. Sift the flour into a bowl and rub in the butter with your fingertips, then stir in half the grated cheese with the chives and seasoning. Add just enough milk to bind the dry ingredients and mix quickly to form a soft dough. Pat out the dough to a round, about 2.5cm/1in thick. Cut it into 12 triangles. Brush with a little milk.

5 Remove the casserole from the oven and stir in the beans. Overlap the triangles on top and sprinkle with the remaining cheese. Return to the oven, uncovered, for 20–25 minutes, or until the scone topping is golden brown and cooked through. Serve immediately.

> **Cook's Tip**
> *Use any of your favourite vegetables, as long as the overall weight remains the same. Firm vegetables may need a little longer cooking.*

Vegetarian Cassoulet

Every town in south-west France has its own version of this popular classic. Serve this hearty vegetable version with warm French bread.

Serves 4–6
400g/14oz/1¾ cups dried haricot (navy) beans, soaked overnight in water to cover
1 bay leaf
1.75 litres/3 pints/7½ cups water
2 onions
3 cloves
5ml/1 tsp olive oil
2 garlic cloves, crushed

2 leeks, thickly sliced
12 baby carrots
115g/4oz/1⅔ cups button (white) mushrooms
400g/14oz can chopped tomatoes
15ml/1 tbsp tomato purée (paste)
5ml/1 tsp paprika
15ml/1 tbsp chopped fresh thyme
30ml/2 tbsp chopped fresh parsley
115g/4oz/2 cups fresh white breadcrumbs
salt and ground black pepper

1 Drain the beans. Rinse them under cold running water, then put them in a large pan. Add the bay leaf, then pour in the water. Bring to the boil and cook rapidly for 10 minutes.

2 Peel one of the onions and spike it with cloves. Add it to the beans and lower the heat. Cover and simmer gently for 1 hour, until the beans are almost tender. Drain, reserving the stock but discarding the bay leaf and onion.

3 Preheat the oven to 160°C/325°F/Gas 3. Chop the remaining onion. Heat the oil in a large flameproof casserole. Add the chopped onion and garlic and cook over a low heat, stirring occasionally, for 5 minutes, or until softened. Add the leeks, carrots, mushrooms, chopped tomatoes, tomato purée, paprika and thyme to the casserole. Stir in 400ml/14fl oz/1⅔ cups of the reserved stock.

4 Bring to the boil, cover and simmer gently for 10 minutes. Stir in the cooked beans and parsley. Season to taste, sprinkle with the fresh breadcrumbs and bake, uncovered, for 35 minutes, or until the topping is golden brown and crisp.

Lentil Dhal with Roasted Garlic

This spicy lentil dhal makes a comforting, starchy meal when served with boiled rice or Indian breads and a vegetable dish.

Serves 4–6

1 head of garlic
30ml/2 tbsp extra virgin olive oil, plus extra for brushing
40g/1½oz/3 tbsp ghee or butter
1 onion, chopped
2 fresh green chillies, seeded and chopped
15ml/1 tbsp chopped fresh root ginger
225g/8oz/1 cup yellow or red split lentils
900ml/1½ pints/3¾ cups water
5ml/1 tsp ground cumin
5ml/1 tsp ground coriander
2 tomatoes, peeled and diced
a little lemon juice
salt and ground black pepper
30–45ml/2–3 tbsp fresh coriander (cilantro) sprigs, to garnish

For the spice mix
30ml/2 tbsp groundnut (peanut) oil
4–5 shallots, sliced
2 garlic cloves, thinly sliced
15g/½oz/1 tbsp ghee or butter
5ml/1 tsp cumin seeds
5ml/1 tsp mustard seeds
3–4 small dried red chillies
8–10 fresh curry leaves

1 Preheat the oven to 180°C/350°F/Gas 4. Place the garlic in an oiled roasting pan and roast it whole for 30 minutes.

2 Meanwhile, melt the ghee or butter in a large pan. Add the onion, fresh chillies and ginger and cook over a low heat, stirring occasionally, for 10 minutes, until golden.

3 Stir in the lentils and water. Bring to the boil, then lower the heat and partially cover the pan. Simmer, stirring occasionally, for about 35 minutes, until the mixture looks like a very thick soup.

4 When the garlic is soft and tender, remove it from the oven and let it cool slightly. Cut off the top third and, holding the garlic over a bowl, dig out the flesh from each clove so that it drops into the bowl. Mash it to a paste with the oil.

5 Stir the roasted garlic purée, cumin and ground coriander into the lentil mixture and season with salt and pepper. Cook for 10 minutes stirring frequently. Stir in the diced tomatoes, then adjust the seasoning, adding a little lemon juice to taste.

6 For the spice mix, heat the oil in a small, heavy pan and cook the shallots until crisp and browned. Add the garlic and cook until it colours slightly. Remove the mixture from the pan and set it aside.

7 Melt the ghee or butter in the same pan and fry the cumin and mustard seeds until the mustard seeds pop. Stir in the dried chillies, curry leaves and the shallot mixture, then swirl the hot mixture into the cooked dhal. Garnish with the coriander sprigs and serve immediately.

> **Cook's Tip**
> Do not be alarmed by the quantity of garlic; when roasted, it acquires a mild and mellow flavour.

Tomato & Lentil Dhal with Toasted Almonds

Richly flavoured with spices, coconut milk and tomatoes, this lentil dish is good enough to serve as part of a celebration supper.

Serves 4

30ml/2 tbsp vegetable oil
1 large onion, finely chopped
3 garlic cloves, chopped
1 carrot, diced
10ml/2 tsp cumin seeds
10ml/2 tsp yellow mustard seeds
2.5cm/1in piece of fresh root ginger, grated
10ml/2 tsp ground turmeric
5ml/1 tsp mild chilli powder
5ml/1 tsp garam masala
225g/8oz/1 cup red split lentils
400ml/14fl oz/1⅔ cups water
400ml/14fl oz/1⅔ cups coconut milk
5 tomatoes, peeled, seeded and chopped
juice of 2 limes
60ml/4 tbsp chopped fresh coriander (cilantro)
salt and ground black pepper
25g/1oz/¼ cup flaked (sliced) almonds, toasted, to serve

1 Heat the oil in a large, heavy pan. Sauté the onion over a low heat, stirring occasionally, for 5 minutes, until softened. Add the garlic, carrot, cumin and mustard seeds and ginger. Cook for 5 minutes, stirring constantly, until the seeds begin to pop and the carrot softens slightly.

2 Stir in the ground turmeric, chilli powder and garam masala, and cook for 1 minute, or until the flavours begin to mingle, stirring to prevent the spices from burning.

3 Add the lentils, water, coconut milk and tomatoes and season well with salt and pepper. Bring to the boil, then lower the heat, cover and simmer for about 15 minutes, stirring occasionally to prevent the lentils from sticking.

4 Stir in the lime juice and 45ml/3 tbsp of the fresh coriander and check the seasoning. Cook for 10–15 minutes more, until the lentils are tender. Spoon into a warmed serving dish and sprinkle with the remaining coriander and the toasted flaked almonds. Serve immediately.

Chickpea Stew

This hearty chickpea and vegetable stew makes a filling meal.

Serves 4
30ml/2 tbsp olive oil
1 small onion, chopped
225g/8oz carrots, halved and thinly sliced
2.5ml/ ½ tsp ground cumin
5ml/1 tsp ground coriander
30ml/2 tbsp plain (all-purpose) flour

225g/8oz courgettes (zucchini), halved lengthways and sliced
200g/7oz can corn kernels, drained
400g/14oz can chickpeas, drained and rinsed
30ml/2 tbsp tomato purée (paste)
200ml/7fl oz/scant 1 cup hot Vegetable Stock
salt and ground black pepper
garlic-flavoured mashed potato, to serve (optional)

1 Heat the oil in a frying pan. Add the onion and carrots. Toss to coat the vegetables in the oil, then cook over a medium heat, stirring occasionally, for 4 minutes.

2 Stir in the ground cumin, coriander and flour. Cook, stirring constantly, for 1 minute.

3 Add the courgette slices to the pan with the corn, chickpeas, tomato purée and vegetable stock. Stir well. Cook for about 10 minutes, stirring frequently.

4 Taste the stew and season with salt and pepper. Serve with garlic-flavoured mashed potato (see Cook's Tip), if you like.

Cook's Tip
For speedy garlic-flavoured mashed potatoes, simply mash 675g/1½lb boiled potatoes with garlic butter and stir in chopped fresh parsley and a little crème fraîche. Alternatively, add 10–12 peeled garlic cloves to the potatoes during cooking and then mash with the potatoes, adding butter, herbs and crème fraîche to taste. This may seem an alarming quantity of garlic, but the flavour is actually quite subtle.

Shepherdess Pie

A no-meat version of the timeless classic, this dish does not contain any dairy products, so it is also suitable for vegans.

Serves 6–8
1kg/2¼lb potatoes
45ml/3 tbsp extra virgin olive oil
45ml/3 tbsp sunflower oil
1 large onion, chopped
1 green (bell) pepper, seeded and chopped
2 carrots, coarsely grated
2 garlic cloves
115g/4oz/1⅔ cups mushrooms, coarsely chopped
2 x 400g/14oz cans aduki beans, drained
600ml/1 pint/2½ cups Vegetable Stock
5ml/1 tsp yeast extract
2 bay leaves
5ml/1 tsp dried mixed herbs
dried breadcrumbs or chopped nuts, for the topping
salt and ground black pepper

1 Bring a large pan of water to the boil. Add the unpeeled potatoes and cook for about 30 minutes, until tender. Drain, reserving a little of the cooking water.

2 As soon as the potatoes are cool enough to handle, remove the skins. Put the skinned potatoes in a bowl and mash them with the olive oil, adding enough of the reserved cooking water to make a smooth purée. Season well with salt and pepper.

3 Heat the sunflower oil in a large, heavy frying pan. Add the chopped onion, green pepper, carrots and garlic and cook over a low heat, stirring occasionally, for about 5 minutes, until the onion is softened.

4 Stir in the mushrooms and beans. Cook for 2 minutes more, then stir in the stock, yeast extract, bay leaves and mixed herbs. Simmer for 15 minutes.

5 Preheat the grill (broiler). Remove and discard the bay leaves from the vegetable and bean mixture, then tip it into a gratin dish. Spoon the mashed potatoes on top and sprinkle the breadcrumbs or chopped nuts over the top. Grill (broil) for 5 minutes, until the topping is golden brown. Serve immediately.

Chilli Beans with Basmati Rice

Red kidney beans, tomatoes and chilli make a great combination. Serve with pasta or pitta bread instead of rice, if you like.

Serves 4

350g/12oz/1¾ cups basmati rice
30ml/2 tbsp olive oil
1 large onion, chopped
1 garlic clove, crushed
15ml/1 tbsp hot chilli powder
15ml/1 tbsp plain (all-purpose) flour
15ml/1 tbsp tomato purée (paste)
400g/14oz can chopped tomatoes
400g/14oz can red kidney beans, drained and rinsed
150ml/¼ pint/⅔ cup hot Vegetable Stock
salt and ground black pepper
chopped fresh parsley, to garnish

1 Rinse the rice several times in cold water. If there is sufficient time, leave it to soak for about 30 minutes.

2 Bring a large pan of water to the boil. Drain the rice, then cook it in the water for 10–12 minutes, until tender.

3 Meanwhile, heat the oil in a heavy frying pan. Add the onion and garlic and cook over a low heat, stirring occasionally, for 2 minutes. Stir in the chilli powder and flour. Cook, stirring frequently, for 2 minutes.

4 Stir in the tomato purée, tomatoes, beans and hot vegetable stock. Cover and cook for 12 minutes, stirring occasionally.

5 Taste the mixture and stir in salt and pepper, if needed. Drain the rice and serve immediately, with the chilli beans, sprinkled with a little chopped fresh parsley.

Cook's Tip
Basmati is generally considered to be the long grain rice with the finest flavour and texture. However, if you prefer to use another type, including brown rice, there is, of course, no reason why you shouldn't.

Red Bean Chilli

White wine and soy sauce may not be standard ingredients in chilli, but they give this spicy bean dish a depth of flavour unmatched by more mundane mixtures.

Serves 4

30ml/2 tbsp vegetable oil
1 onion, chopped
400g/14oz can chopped tomatoes
2 garlic cloves, crushed
300ml/½ pint/1¼ cups white wine
about 300ml/½ pint/1¼ cups Vegetable Stock
115g/4oz/½ cup red split lentils
2 fresh thyme sprigs or 5ml/1 tsp dried thyme
10ml/2 tsp ground cumin
45ml/3 tbsp dark soy sauce
½ fresh hot chilli, seeded and finely chopped
5ml/1 tsp mixed (apple pie) spice
225g/8oz can red kidney beans, drained and rinsed
10ml/2 tsp sugar
salt
boiled rice and corn, to serve

1 Heat the oil in a large, heavy pan. Add the onion and cook over a low heat, stirring occasionally, for about 5 minutes, until slightly softened.

2 Add the tomatoes and garlic, cook for 10 minutes, then stir in the wine and stock. Bring to the boil.

3 Add the lentils, thyme, cumin, soy sauce, chilli and mixed spice. Cover, then simmer for 40 minutes, or until the lentils are cooked, stirring occasionally and adding more water if the lentils begin to dry out.

4 Stir in the kidney beans and sugar and continue cooking for 10 minutes, adding a little extra stock or water if the mixture is becoming too dry. Season to taste with salt and serve hot with boiled rice and corn.

Cook's Tip
If you have a taste for very hot, spicy food, do not seed the chilli before chopping it.

Veggie Burgers

Unlike some commercially-produced veggie burgers, which are decidedly dreary, these are full of flavour.

Serves 4

115g/4oz/1⅔ cups mushrooms, finely chopped
1 small onion, chopped
1 small courgette (zucchini), chopped
1 carrot, chopped
25g/1oz/¼ cup unsalted peanuts
115g/4oz/2 cups fresh breadcrumbs
30ml/2 tbsp chopped fresh parsley
5ml/1 tsp yeast extract
fine oatmeal or flour, for shaping
a little vegetable oil, for frying
salt and ground black pepper
salad, to serve

1 Cook the mushrooms in a non-stick pan without oil, stirring them constantly, for 8–10 minutes to drive off all the moisture.

2 Process the onion, courgette, carrot and nuts in a food processor until the mixture starts to bind together. Scrape it into a bowl.

3 Stir in the mushrooms, breadcrumbs, parsley and yeast extract to taste. Season to taste. Coat your hands and a board with the oatmeal or flour, then shape the mixture into four burgers. Chill in the refrigerator for 30 minutes.

4 Heat a little oil in a non-stick frying pan and cook the burgers for 8–10 minutes, turning once, until they are cooked and golden brown. Serve hot with a crisp salad.

Cook's Tip

These burgers can be cooked on a barbecue, but do not place them directly on the grill, as they are quite delicate and likely to break up. Use a wire rack or foil dish and brush with a little vegetable oil on both sides.

Marinated Tofu Kebabs

Perfect partners for both the vegetarian burgers featured here, these kebabs are very easy to make.

Serves 4

30ml/2 tbsp soy sauce
5ml/1 tsp groundnut (peanut) oil
5ml/1 tsp sesame oil
1 garlic clove, crushed
15ml/1 tbsp grated fresh root ginger
15ml/1 tbsp clear honey
225g/8oz firm tofu, cut into 1cm/½in cubes
2 small courgettes (zucchini), thickly sliced
8 baby (pearl) onions
8 mushrooms

1 Combine the soy sauce, oils, garlic, ginger and honey in a shallow dish. Add the tofu cubes and marinate for 1–2 hours.
2 Drain the tofu, reserving the marinade, and thread on to four long metal skewers, alternating with the vegetables. Brush with the reserved marinade and grill (broil) or cook on a barbecue until golden, turning occasionally.

Red Bean & Mushroom Burgers

Whether you cook these tasty burgers in the kitchen or on the barbecue, they are certain to prove popular with everyone.

Serves 4

15ml/1 tbsp olive oil, plus extra for brushing
1 small onion, finely chopped
1 garlic clove, crushed
5ml/1 tsp ground cumin
5ml/1 tsp ground coriander
2.5ml/½ tsp ground turmeric
115g/4oz/1⅔ cups finely chopped mushrooms
400g/14oz can red kidney beans, drained and rinsed
30ml/2 tbsp chopped fresh coriander (cilantro)
wholemeal (whole-wheat) flour, for forming the burgers
salt and ground black pepper

To serve

warm pitta bread
Greek (US strained plain) yogurt
salad leaves and tomatoes

1 Heat the olive oil in a deep, heavy frying pan. Add the onion and garlic and cook over a medium heat, stirring occasionally, for about 4 minutes, until softened. Add the cumin, ground coriander and turmeric and cook for about 1 minute more, stirring constantly.

2 Add the mushrooms and cook, stirring, until softened and dry. Remove the pan from the heat.

3 Tip the beans into a bowl and then mash them with a fork. Stir them into the mushroom mixture, then add the fresh coriander, mixing thoroughly. Season well with salt and pepper.

4 Using floured hands, form the mixture into four flat burger shapes. If the mixture is too sticky to handle, mix in a little flour. Preheat the grill (broiler).

5 Brush the burgers with olive oil and grill (broil) them for 8–10 minutes, turning once, until golden brown. Alternatively, cook on the barbecue, using a wire rack to turn them easily.

6 Serve immediately with warm pitta bread, Greek yogurt, crisp green salad leaves and tomatoes.

Vegetable Fajitas

A colourful medley of mushrooms and peppers in a spicy sauce, wrapped in tortillas and served with creamy guacamole.

Serves 2

1 onion, sliced
1 red (bell) pepper, seeded and sliced
1 green (bell) pepper, seeded and sliced
1 yellow (bell) pepper, seeded and sliced
1 garlic clove, crushed
225g/8oz/3¼ cups mushrooms, sliced

90ml/6 tbsp vegetable oil
30ml/2 tbsp medium chilli powder
6 warm wheat flour tortillas
salt and ground black pepper
fresh coriander (cilantro) sprigs and lime wedges, to garnish

For the guacamole
1 ripe avocado
1 shallot, coarsely chopped
1 fresh green chilli, seeded and coarsely chopped
juice of 1 lime

1 Combine the onion and red, green and yellow peppers in a large bowl. Add the garlic and mushrooms and mix lightly. Mix the oil and chilli powder in a cup, pour over the vegetable mixture and stir well. Set aside.

2 To make the guacamole, cut the avocado in half lengthways and remove the stone (pit). Scoop the flesh into a food processor or blender and add the shallot, chilli and lime juice. Process for 1 minute, until smooth. Scrape the guacamole into a bowl, cover with clear film (plastic wrap) and chill until required.

3 Heat a large, heavy frying pan or wok until very hot. Add the marinated vegetables and stir-fry over a high heat for 5–6 minutes, until the mushrooms and peppers are just tender. Season well with salt and pepper.

4 Spoon a little of the filling on to each warm tortilla and roll up. Place three fajitas on each of two individual serving plates, garnishing them with the fresh coriander and lime wedges. Offer the guacamole separately.

Black Bean Burritos

Some of the world's most delectable vegetarian dishes come from Mexico. Burritos make a delicious supper.

Serves 4

225g/8oz/1 cup dried black beans, soaked overnight
1 bay leaf
30ml/2 tbsp coarse salt
oil, for greasing

1 small red onion, finely chopped
225g/8oz/2 cups grated Cheddar cheese
15–45ml/1–3 tbsp chopped pickled jalapeño chillies
15ml/1 tbsp chopped fresh coriander (cilantro)
900ml/1½ pints/3¾ cups ready-made tomato salsa
8 wheat flour tortillas
diced avocado and salad, to serve

1 Drain the beans and put them in a large pan. Add fresh cold water to cover and the bay leaf. Bring to the boil, then lower the heat, and simmer, covered, for 30 minutes. Add the salt and continue to simmer for about 30 minutes, until tender. Drain and tip into a bowl. Discard the bay leaf and leave to cool.

2 Preheat the oven to 180°C/350°F/Gas 4. Lightly grease a rectangular ovenproof dish. Add the onion, half the cheese, the jalapeños and coriander to the beans, with 250ml/8fl oz/1 cup of the salsa. Stir and taste for seasoning.

3 Place one tortilla on a board. Spread a spoonful of the filling down the middle, then roll up. Place the burrito in the prepared dish, seam-side down. Repeat with the remaining tortillas.

4 Sprinkle the remaining cheese over the burritos, in a line down the middle. Bake for about 15 minutes, until the cheese melts. Serve the burritos immediately, with diced avocado, salad and the remaining salsa.

> **Variation**
> • Use passata (bottled strained tomatoes) if you don't have any ready-made salsa. Add some chopped onion and diced (bell) peppers to the portion used as a serving sauce.

SPECIAL OCCASION DISHES

One of the first things we think of when there is cause for celebration or friends are to visit is preparing a special meal. This is true throughout the world, as this international collection of sparkling recipes amply demonstrates with festive dishes from France, Italy, Thailand, Turkey, Morocco and many other places. Birthdays and anniversaries, friendly get togethers and family gatherings, whether formal or informal, require some advance preparation if the occasion is to be fun for both guests and hosts.

Cooking a special meal is part of the pleasure and should never become a chore, so these recipes are all easy to follow and none of them involves endless hours of difficult toil or even prohibitively expensive ingredients. Rather, they feature subtle combinations of flavours, textures and colours to delight the eye as well as the taste buds. There are dishes for all seasons and tastes, from the sensational, light as-air Spinach & Wild Mushroom Soufflé to the elegant simplicity of Saffron Risotto. These recipes will also be welcome to cooks whose guests include non-vegetarians. Even dedicated carnivores would find it hard to resist a traditional Chestnut, Stilton & Ale Pie or spicy Thai Vegetable Curry. Indeed, this whole chapter is a celebration itself of the very best of vegetarian cuisine.

Spinach & Wild Mushroom Soufflé

A variety of wild mushrooms combine especially well with eggs and spinach in this sensational soufflé.

Serves 4

50g/2oz/ ¼ cup butter, plus extra for greasing
30ml/2 tbsp freshly grated Parmesan cheese
225g/8oz fresh spinach leaves
1 garlic clove, crushed
175g/6oz/2½ cups assorted wild mushrooms, chopped
200ml/7fl oz/scant 1 cup milk
25g/1oz/ ¼ cup plain (all-purpose flour
6 eggs, separated
pinch of freshly grated nutmeg
salt and ground black pepper

1 Preheat the oven to 190°C/375°F/Gas 5. Butter a 900ml/ 1½ pint/3¾ cup soufflé dish, paying particular attention to the sides. Sprinkle with a little of the cheese. Set aside.

2 Steam the spinach over a medium heat for 3–4 minutes. Cool under cold running water, then drain. Press out as much liquid as you can with the back of a large spoon, squeeze with your hands and then chop finely.

3 Melt the butter in a pan and gently soften the garlic and mushrooms. Increase the heat and cook until the mixture is quite dry. Add the spinach and transfer to a bowl. Cover and keep warm.

4 Measure 45ml/3 tbsp of the milk into a bowl and stir in the flour and egg yolks. Bring the remaining milk to the boil, whisk it into the egg and flour mixture until smooth, then pour the mixture back into the pan and whisk over the heat until the sauce thickens. Stir in the spinach mixture. Season to taste with salt, pepper and grated nutmeg.

5 Whisk the egg whites to form soft peaks. Stir a spoonful into the spinach mixture to lighten it, then fold in the rest.

6 Pour the mixture into the soufflé dish, level the surface, sprinkle with the remaining cheese and bake for about 25 minutes, until well risen and golden. Serve immediately.

Classic Cheese Soufflé

A melt-in-the-mouth cheese soufflé makes one of the most delightful light lunches imaginable. All you need to go with it is salad and a glass of good wine.

Serves 2–3

50g/2oz/ ¼ cup butter
30–45ml/2–3 tbsp fine, dried breadcrumbs
30g/1¼oz/5 tbsp plain (all-purpose) flour
pinch of cayenne pepper
2.5ml/ ½ tsp English (hot) mustard powder
250ml/8fl oz/1 cup milk
50g/2oz/ ½ cup grated mature (sharp) Cheddar cheese
25g/1oz/ ⅓ cup freshly grated Parmesan cheese
4 eggs, separated, plus 1 egg white
salt and ground black pepper

1 Preheat the oven to 190°C/375°F/Gas 5. Melt 15g/ ½oz/ 1 tbsp of the butter and grease a 1.2 litre/2 pint/5 cup soufflé dish. Coat the inside of the dish with the breadcrumbs.

2 Melt the remaining butter in a pan, stir in the flour, cayenne and mustard and cook for 1 minute. Add the milk, whisking constantly, until the mixture boils and thickens to a smooth sauce. Simmer the sauce for 1–2 minutes, then remove from the heat and whisk in all the Cheddar, half the Parmesan and season to taste. Cool a little, then beat in the egg yolks.

3 Whisk the egg whites to soft, glossy peaks. Add a few spoonfuls to the sauce to lighten it. Beat well, then gently fold in the rest of the whites.

4 Pour the mixture into the soufflé dish, level the surface and sprinkle the remaining Parmesan over. Place the dish on a baking sheet and bake for about 25 minutes, until well risen.

Cook's Tip

To help the soufflé rise evenly, run your finger around the inside rim of the dish before baking.

Thai Vegetable Curry

Aubergine & Sweet Potato Stew

Inspired by Thai cooking, this dish has a fragrant coconut sauce.

Serves 6

60ml/4 tbsp groundnut
  (peanut) oil
450g/1lb baby aubergines
  (eggplant), halved
225g/8oz shallots
5ml/1 tsp fennel seeds,
  lightly crushed
4–5 garlic cloves, thinly sliced
25ml/5 tsp finely chopped fresh
  root ginger
475ml/16fl oz/2 cups
  Vegetable Stock
2 lemon grass stalks, outer layers
  discarded, finely chopped

15g/½ oz/½ cup fresh
  coriander (cilantro), stalks and
  leaves chopped separately
3 kaffir lime leaves, lightly bruised
2–3 small fresh red chillies
45–60ml/3–4 tbsp Thai green
  curry paste
675g/1½ lb sweet potatoes,
  peeled and cut into chunks
400ml/14fl oz/1⅔ cups
  coconut milk
2.5–5ml/½–1 tsp light
  muscovado (brown) sugar
250g/9oz/3⅔ cups mushrooms,
  thickly sliced
juice of 1 lime
salt and ground black pepper
fresh basil leaves, to serve

1 Heat half the oil in a wide pan and cook the aubergines, stirring occasionally, until lightly browned on all sides. Remove with a slotted spoon and set aside. Slice four of the shallots and set them aside. Cook the remaining whole shallots in the oil remaining in the pan, until lightly browned. Set aside.

2 Add the remaining oil to the pan and cook the sliced shallots, fennel seeds, garlic and ginger until soft. Add the stock, lemon grass, chopped coriander stalks and any roots, lime leaves and whole chillies. Cover and simmer over a low heat for 5 minutes.

3 Stir in 30ml/2 tbsp of the curry paste and the sweet potatoes. Simmer for 10 minutes, then return the aubergines and shallots to the pan and cook for 5 minutes more. Stir in the coconut milk and sugar. Stir in the mushrooms and simmer for 5 minutes, or until all the vegetables are cooked. Season and add more curry paste and lime juice to taste. Stir in the coriander leaves, sprinkle basil leaves over and serve.

Making your own spice paste gives this curry an authentic flavour.

Serves 4

10ml/2 tsp vegetable oil
400ml/14fl oz/1⅔ cups
  coconut milk
300ml/½ pint/1¼ cups
  Vegetable Stock
225g/8oz new potatoes, halved
  if large
130g/4½ oz baby corn cobs
5ml/1 tsp golden caster
  (superfine) sugar
175g/6oz broccoli florets
1 red (bell) pepper, seeded and
  sliced lengthways
115g/4oz spinach, tough stalks
  removed and shredded
salt and ground black pepper

30ml/2 tbsp chopped fresh
  coriander (cilantro), to garnish
cooked jasmine rice, to serve

For the spice paste

1 fresh red chilli, seeded
  and chopped
3 fresh green chillies, seeded
  and chopped
1 lemon grass stalk, outer layers
  discarded and finely chopped
2 shallots, chopped
finely grated rind of 1 lime
2 garlic cloves, chopped
5ml/1 tsp ground coriander
2.5ml/½ tsp ground cumin
1cm/½in piece of fresh galangal
  or root ginger, finely chopped
30ml/2 tbsp chopped fresh
  coriander (cilantro)

1 First, make the spice paste. Place all the ingredients in a food processor or blender and process to a coarse paste.

2 Heat the oil in a large, heavy pan and fry the spice paste for 1–2 minutes, stirring constantly. Add the coconut milk and stock, and bring to the boil.

3 Lower the heat, add the potatoes and simmer gently for 15 minutes. Add the baby corn cobs, season to taste with salt and pepper and cook for 2 minutes. Stir in the sugar, broccoli and red pepper and cook for 2 minutes more, until the vegetables are tender.

4 Stir in the shredded spinach and half the fresh coriander. Cook for 2 minutes. Serve over jasmine rice, garnished with the remaining chopped coriander.

Baked Peppers with Egg & Lentils

A breadcrumb or rice filling is commonly used for peppers. Lentils make a delicious change and the eggs add extra protein.

Serves 4
75g/3oz/scant ½ cup Puy lentils
2.5ml/ ½ tsp ground turmeric
2.5ml/ ½ tsp ground coriander
2.5ml/ ½ tsp paprika
450ml/ ¾ pint/scant 2 cups
  Vegetable Stock
2 large (bell) peppers, halved
  lengthways and seeded
a little vegetable oil
15ml/1 tbsp chopped fresh mint
4 eggs
salt and ground black pepper
fresh coriander (cilantro) sprigs,
  to garnish

1 Put the lentils in a pan with the spices and stock. Bring to the boil, stirring occasionally, then lower the heat and simmer for 30–40 minutes. If necessary, add some water during cooking.

2 Preheat the oven to 190°C/375°F/Gas 4. Brush the peppers lightly with oil and place them close together, cut sides upwards, in a roasting pan. Stir the mint into the lentils, then fill the peppers with the mixture.

3 Beat one egg in a small jug (pitcher) and carefully pour it over the lentil mixture in one of the peppers. Using a small spoon, gently stir it into the lentils and season with salt and pepper to taste. Repeat with the remaining eggs and peppers. Bake for 10 minutes, garnish with coriander and serve.

Variations
• Add a little extra flavour to the lentil mixture by mixing in chopped onion and tomatoes sautéed in olive oil before filling the (bell) peppers.
• Use beefsteak tomatoes instead of peppers. Cut a lid off the tomatoes and scoop out the flesh with a teaspoon. Fill with the lentils and egg and bake.
• For an extra touch of spice, add one or two finely chopped fresh green chillies to the lentils.

Onions Stuffed with Goat's Cheese & Sun-dried Tomatoes

Roasted onions and creamy goat's cheese truly are a winning combination.

Serves 4
4 large onions
oil, for greasing
150g/5oz goat's cheese, crumbled
50g/2oz/1 cup fresh breadcrumbs
8 sun-dried tomatoes in olive oil,
  drained and chopped
1–2 garlic cloves, finely chopped
2.5ml/ ½ tsp chopped
  fresh thyme
30ml/2 tbsp chopped
  fresh parsley, plus extra
  to garnish
1 small (US medium) egg, beaten
45ml/3 tbsp pine nuts, toasted
30ml/2 tbsp olive oil (from
  the tomatoes)
salt and ground black pepper

1 Bring a large pan of lightly salted water to the boil. Add the whole onions in their skins and boil for 10 minutes. Drain and cool, then cut each onion in half horizontally and peel.

2 Using a teaspoon to scoop out the flesh, remove the centre of each onion, leaving a thick shell. Reserve the flesh and place the shells in an oiled ovenproof dish. Preheat the oven to 190°C/375°F/Gas 5.

3 Chop the scooped-out onion flesh and place it in a bowl. Add the goat's cheese, breadcrumbs, sun-dried tomatoes, garlic, thyme, parsley and egg. Mix well, then season to taste with salt and pepper. Add the toasted pine nuts.

4 Divide the stuffing among the onions and cover with foil. Bake for about 25 minutes. Uncover, drizzle with the oil and cook for 30–40 minutes more, until bubbling and well cooked. Baste occasionally during cooking. Serve, garnished with parsley.

Variation
Omit the goat's cheese and add 115g/4oz/1⅔ cups finely chopped mushrooms and 1 grated carrot.

Baked Stuffed Squash

A creamy, sweet and nutty mixture makes the perfect filling for tender squash.

Serves 4

2 butternut or acorn squash, about 500g/1¼ lb each
15ml/1 tbsp olive oil
175g/6oz/1 cup drained canned corn kernels
115g/4oz/½ cup unsweetened chestnut purée
75ml/5 tbsp low-fat natural (plain) yogurt
50g/2oz fresh goat's cheese
salt and ground black pepper
chopped chives, to garnish
mixed salad leaves, to serve

1 Preheat the oven to 180°C/350°F/Gas 4. Cut the squash in half lengthwise, scoop out the seeds and place the halves, skin-side down, on a baking sheet.

2 Brush the squash flesh lightly with the olive oil, then bake for about 30 minutes.

3 Meanwhile, mix the corn, chestnut purée and yogurt in a bowl. Season to taste with salt and pepper.

4 Remove the squash from the oven and divide the chestnut mixture between them, spooning it into the hollows.

5 Top each half with one-quarter of the goat's cheese and return to the oven for 10–15 minutes. Garnish with chopped chives and serve immediately with salad leaves.

Variations
• Use mozzarella or other mild, soft cheeses in place of the goat's cheese. The cheese can be omitted entirely for a lower-fat alternative.
• Add 15–30ml/1–2 tbsp finely chopped nuts, such as almonds or pistachios to the filling.
• This filling also goes well with courgettes (zucchini). Cut six large courgettes in half lengthways and bake for 20 minutes.

Stuffed Mushrooms with Pine Nut Tarator

Portabello mushrooms have a rich flavour and a meaty texture. They go well with this fragrant and tasty herb and lemon stuffing.

Serves 4–6

45ml/3 tbsp olive oil, plus extra for brushing
1 onion, finely chopped
2 garlic cloves, crushed
30ml/2 tbsp chopped fresh thyme or 5ml/1 tsp dried thyme
8 portabello mushrooms, stalks removed and finely chopped
400g/14oz can aduki beans, drained and rinsed
50g/2oz/1 cup fresh wholemeal (whole-wheat) breadcrumbs
juice of 1 lemon
185g/6½ oz goat's cheese, crumbled
salt and ground black pepper

For the pine nut tarator
50g/2oz/½ cup pine nuts, toasted
50g/2oz/1 cup cubed white bread
2 garlic cloves, chopped
200ml/7fl oz/scant 1 cup milk
45ml/3 tbsp olive oil

1 Preheat the oven to 200°C/400°F/Gas 6. Heat the oil in a large, heavy frying pan. Add the onion and garlic and cook over a low heat, stirring occasionally, for 5 minutes, until softened. Add the thyme and chopped mushroom stalks and cook for 3 minutes more, stirring occasionally, until tender.

2 Stir the aduki beans into the mixture with the breadcrumbs and lemon juice, season well with salt and pepper, then cook for 2 minutes, until heated through.

3 Remove the pan from the heat and, using a fork or potato masher, mash the mixture until about two-thirds of the beans are broken up, leaving the remaining beans whole.

4 Brush an ovenproof dish and the tops and sides of the mushroom caps with oil. Place them, gills uppermost, in the dish and top each one with a spoonful of the bean mixture. Cover with foil and bake for 20 minutes.

5 Remove the foil. Top each mushroom with goat's cheese and bake for 15 minutes more, or until the cheese has melted and the mushrooms are tender.

6 Meanwhile, make the pine nut tarator. Put the pine nuts, bread and garlic in a food processor and process briefly. Add the milk and olive oil and process until creamy. Serve the tarator with the mushrooms.

Cook's Tip
Use dried beans if you prefer. Soak 200g/7oz/1 cup beans overnight in cold water, then drain and rinse well. Place in a pan with water to cover and boil rapidly for 10 minutes. Reduce the heat, cook for 30 minutes, until tender, then drain. Alternatively, cover the dried beans with boiling water and leave to soak for about 3 hours before draining and cooking.

Aubergine Parmigiana

A classic Italian dish, in which blissfully tender sliced aubergines are layered with melting creamy mozzarella, fresh Parmesan and a good home-made tomato sauce.

Serves 4–6
3 medium aubergines (eggplant), thinly sliced
olive oil, for brushing
300g/11oz mozzarella cheese, sliced
115g/4oz/1⅓ cups freshly grated Parmesan cheese
30–45ml/2–3 tbsp natural-coloured dried breadcrumbs
salt and ground black pepper
fresh basil sprigs, to garnish

For the sauce
30ml/2 tbsp olive oil
1 onion, finely chopped
2 garlic cloves, crushed
400g/14oz can chopped tomatoes
5ml/1 tsp sugar
about 6 fresh basil leaves

1 Layer the aubergine slices in a colander, sprinkling each layer with a little salt. Drain for about 20 minutes, then rinse under cold running water and pat dry with kitchen paper.

2 Preheat the oven to 200°C/400°F/Gas 6. Lay the aubergine slices on non-stick baking sheets, brush the tops with olive oil and bake for 10–15 minutes until softened.

3 Meanwhile, make the sauce. Heat the oil in a pan. Add the onion and garlic and cook over a low heat, stirring occasionally, for 5 minutes. Add the canned tomatoes and sugar and season with salt and pepper to taste. Bring to the boil, then lower the heat and simmer for about 10 minutes, until reduced and thickened. Tear the basil leaves into small pieces and stir them into the sauce.

4 Layer the aubergines in a greased shallow ovenproof dish with the sliced mozzarella, the tomato sauce and the grated Parmesan, ending with a layer of Parmesan mixed with the breadcrumbs. Bake for 20–25 minutes, until golden brown and bubbling. Allow to stand for 5 minutes before cutting. Serve garnished with basil.

Savoy Cabbage Stuffed with Mushroom Barley

The veined texture of Savoy cabbage provides good cover for a hearty stuffing of barley and wild mushrooms.

Serves 4
50g/2oz/¼ cup butter
2 medium onions, chopped
1 celery stick, sliced
225g/8oz/3¼ cups assorted wild and cultivated mushrooms
175g/6oz/¾ cup pearl barley
1 fresh thyme sprig
750ml/1¼ pints/3 cups water
30ml/2 tbsp cashew nut butter
½ vegetable stock (bouillon) cube
1 Savoy cabbage
salt and ground black pepper

1 Melt the butter in a large pan and cook the onions and celery over a low heat, stirring occasionally, for 5 minutes, until soft. Add the mushrooms and cook until they release their juices, then add the barley, thyme, water and the nut butter. Bring to the boil, lower the heat, cover and simmer for 30 minutes. Crumble in the stock cube, cover again and simmer for 20 minutes more. Season to taste with salt and pepper.

2 Separate the cabbage leaves and cut away the thick stem. Blanch the leaves in a pan of lightly salted boiling water for 3–4 minutes. Drain, refresh under cold running water and then drain well again.

3 Lay a 45cm/18in square of muslin (cheesecloth) over a steaming basket. Line the muslin with large cabbage leaves. Spread a layer of mushroom barley over the leaves.

4 Cover with a second layer of leaves and filling. Continue until the centre is full. Draw together opposite corners of the muslin and tie firmly.

5 Set the steaming basket in a pan containing 2.5cm/1in of simmering water. Cover and steam for 30 minutes.

6 To serve, place on a warmed serving plate, untie the muslin and carefully pull it away from underneath the cabbage.

Turkish-style New Potato Casserole

A one-pot baked dish that's both easy to make and tastes delicious – who could ask for more?

Serves 4

60ml/4 tbsp olive oil
1 large onion, chopped
2 small–medium aubergines (eggplant), cut into small cubes
4 courgettes (zucchini), cut into small chunks
1 green (bell) pepper, seeded and chopped
1 red or yellow (bell) pepper, seeded and chopped
115g/4oz/1 cup fresh or frozen peas
115g/4oz green beans
450g/1lb new potatoes, cubed
2.5ml/ ½ tsp cinnamon
2.5ml/ ½ tsp ground cumin
5ml/1 tsp paprika
4–5 tomatoes, halved, seeded and chopped
400g/14oz can chopped tomatoes
30ml/2 tbsp chopped fresh parsley
3–4 garlic cloves, crushed
350ml/12fl oz/1 ½ cups Vegetable Stock
salt and ground black pepper
black olives and fresh parsley, to garnish

1 Preheat the oven to 190°C/375°F/Gas 5. Heat 45ml/3 tbsp of the oil in a heavy pan. Add the onion and cook over a medium heat, stirring occasionally, for 5–7 minutes, until golden.

2 Add the aubergines, sauté for about 3 minutes, then add the courgettes, peppers, peas, beans and potatoes. Stir in the cinnamon, cumin and paprika and season to taste with salt and pepper. Continue to cook for 3 minutes, stirring constantly. Transfer to a shallow ovenproof dish.

3 Mix the fresh and canned tomatoes in a bowl. Stir in the parsley, garlic and the remaining olive oil.

4 Pour the stock over the aubergine mixture, and spoon the prepared tomato mixture over the top.

5 Cover with foil and bake for 30–45 minutes, until the vegetables are tender. Serve immediately, garnished with black olives and parsley.

Spicy Potato Strudel

Take a tasty mixture of vegetables in a spicy, creamy sauce and wrap in crisp filo pastry for a stylish and satisfying main course.

Serves 4

65g/2½ oz/5 tbsp butter
1 onion, chopped
2 carrots, coarsely grated
1 courgette (zucchini), chopped
350g/12oz firm potatoes, finely chopped
10ml/2 tsp mild curry paste
2.5ml/ ½ tsp dried thyme
150ml/ ¼ pint/ ⅔ cup water
1 egg, beaten
30ml/2 tbsp single (light) cream
50g/2oz/ ½ cup grated Cheddar cheese
8 sheets filo pastry, thawed if frozen
sesame seeds, for sprinkling
salt and ground black pepper
lamb's lettuce (corn salad), to garnish

1 Melt 25g/1oz/2 tbsp of the butter in a large frying pan and cook the onion, carrots, courgette and potatoes for 5 minutes, tossing them frequently so that they cook evenly. Stir in the curry paste and continue to cook the vegetables, stirring frequently, for 1–2 minutes more.

2 Add the thyme and water and season with salt and pepper to taste. Bring to the boil, then lower the heat and simmer for 10 minutes, until tender, stirring occasionally.

3 Remove the pan from the heat and tip the mixture into a large bowl. When cool, mix in the egg, cream and cheese. Chill until ready to fill the filo pastry.

4 Preheat the oven to 190°C/375°F/Gas 5. Melt the remaining butter. Lay out four sheets of filo pastry, slightly overlapping them to form a fairly large rectangle. Brush with some melted butter and fit the other sheets on top. Brush again.

5 Spoon the filling along one long side, then roll up the pastry. Form it into a circle and set on a baking sheet. Brush again with the last of the butter and sprinkle over the sesame seeds. Bake for about 25 minutes, until golden and crisp. Leave to stand for 5 minutes before cutting. Garnish with lamb's lettuce.

Cheese & Onion Quiche

Perfect for picnics, parties and family suppers, this classic quiche celebrates a timeless combination.

Serves 6–8
200g/7oz/1¾ cups plain (all-purpose flour
2.5ml/ ½ tsp salt
90g/3½ oz/scant ½ cup butter
about 60ml/4 tbsp iced water

For the filling
25g/1oz/2 tbsp butter
1 large onion, thinly sliced
3 eggs
300ml/ ½ pint/1¼ cups single (light) cream
1.5ml/ ¼ tsp freshly grated nutmeg
90g/3½ oz/scant 1 cup grated hard cheese, such as mature (sharp) Cheddar or Gruyère
salt and ground black pepper

1 To make the pastry, sift the flour and salt into a bowl. Rub in the butter with your fingertips, then add enough iced water to make a firm dough. Knead lightly, wrap in clear film (plastic wrap) and chill in the refrigerator for 20 minutes.

2 Roll out the dough and line a 23cm/9in loose-based flan tin (quiche pan). Prick the pastry base a few times. Line the pastry with foil and baking beans and chill again for about 15 minutes.

3 Preheat the oven to 200°C/400°F/Gas 6. Place a baking sheet in the oven. Stand the flan tin on the baking sheet and bake blind for 15 minutes. Remove the beans and foil and return the pastry case to the oven for 5 minutes more. Reduce the oven temperature to 180°C/350°F/Gas 4.

4 To make the filling, melt the butter in a heavy frying pan. Add the onion and cook over a low heat, stirring occasionally, for 5 minutes, until softened. Beat together the eggs and cream. Add the nutmeg and season with salt and pepper.

5 Spoon the onion mixture into the cooked pastry case and sprinkle over the grated cheese. Pour in the egg and cream mixture. Bake for 35–40 minutes, or until the filling has just set. Cool, then ease the quiche out of the tin to serve.

Mushroom Tart

A mixture of fresh wild mushrooms is best for this simple tart, but if the only mushrooms you can find are cultivated, it is still well worth making.

Serves 4
350g/12oz shortcrust pastry, thawed if frozen
50g/2oz/ ¼ cup butter
3 onions, halved and sliced

350g/12oz/4 cups mushrooms, such as portabello, ceps and oyster mushrooms, sliced
leaves from 1 fresh thyme sprig, chopped
pinch of freshly grated nutmeg
45ml/3 tbsp milk
60ml/4 tbsp single (light) cream
1 egg, plus 2 egg yolks
salt and ground black pepper

1 Roll out the pastry on a lightly floured surface and line a 23cm/9in loose-based flan tin (quiche pan). Place the flan case (pie shell) in the refrigerator to rest for about 1 hour.

2 Preheat the oven to 190°C/375°F/Gas 5. Prick the pastry base a few times with a fork, then line the flan case with foil and fill it with baking beans. Place on a baking sheet and bake blind for 25 minutes. Remove from the oven, lift out the paper and baking beans and leave the case to cool without removing it from the tin.

3 Melt the butter in a heavy frying pan, add the sliced onions, cover and cook over a very low heat, stirring occasionally, for about 20 minutes, until very soft and beginning to caramelize. Add the sliced mushrooms and thyme leaves and continue cooking, stirring occasionally, for a further 10 minutes. Season to taste with salt, freshly ground black pepper and nutmeg.

4 Mix the milk and cream in a jug (pitcher) and beat in the egg and egg yolks. Spoon the mushroom mixture into the flan case and level the surface. Pour over the milk and egg mixture. Bake for 15–20 minutes, until the centre is just firm to the touch. Cool slightly, then gently ease the tart out of the tin and place it on a plate for serving.

Mediterranean One-crust Pie

This free-form pie encases a rich tomato, aubergine and kidney bean filling. If your pastry cracks, just patch it up – it adds to the pie's rustic character.

Serves 4

500g/1¼lb aubergines (eggplant), cubed
1 red (bell) pepper
30ml/2 tbsp olive oil, plus extra for greasing
1 large onion, finely chopped
1 courgette (zucchini), sliced
2 garlic cloves, crushed
15ml/1 tbsp chopped fresh oregano, plus extra to garnish
200g/7oz can red kidney beans, drained and rinsed
115g/4oz/1 cup pitted black olives, rinsed
150ml/¼ pint/⅔ cup passata (bottled strained tomatoes)
beaten egg, for brushing
30ml/2 tbsp semolina
salt and ground black pepper

For the pastry

75g/3oz/⅔ cup plain (all-purpose) flour
75g/3oz/⅔ cup wholemeal (whole-wheat) flour
75g/3oz/6 tbsp margarine
50g/2oz/⅔ cup freshly grated Parmesan cheese

1 Preheat the oven to 220°C/425°F/Gas 7. Make the pastry. Sift both types of flour into a large bowl and tip the bran remaining in the sieve into the bowl. Rub in the margarine with a pastry blender or your fingertips until the mixture resembles fine breadcrumbs, then stir in the grated Parmesan. Mix in enough cold water to form a soft dough. Shape into a ball, wrap and chill for 30 minutes.

2 Meanwhile, place the aubergine cubes in a colander, sprinkle with salt, then leave to drain in the sink for about 30 minutes. Rinse well, drain and pat dry with kitchen paper.

3 Meanwhile, grill (broil) the red pepper until blistered and charred all over. Put in a small bowl, cover with crumpled kitchen paper and leave to cool slightly. Rub off the skin, remove the core and seeds and dice the flesh. Set it aside.

4 Heat the oil in a large, heavy frying pan. Add the onion and cook over a low heat, stirring occasionally, for 5 minutes, until softened. Add the aubergine cubes and cook for about 5 minutes, until tender.

5 Stir in the courgette slices, garlic and oregano and cook for a further 5 minutes, stirring frequently. Add the kidney beans and olives, stir well to mix, then add the passata and diced red pepper. Season to taste with salt and pepper. Cook over a medium heat, stirring occasionally, until heated through, then set aside to cool.

6 Roll out the pastry to a rough 30cm/12in round. Place on a lightly oiled baking sheet. Brush with some beaten egg, then sprinkle over the semolina, leaving a 4cm/1½in border. Spoon over the filling.

7 Gather up the edges of the pastry to partly cover the filling – it should remain open in the middle. Brush with the remaining egg and bake for 30–35 minutes, until golden. Transfer to a warmed serving plate, garnish with oregano and serve.

Chestnut, Stilton & Ale Pie

This hearty winter dish has a rich stout gravy and a herb pastry top.

Serves 4

30ml/2 tbsp sunflower oil
2 large onions, chopped
500g/1¼lb/8 cups button (white) mushrooms, halved
3 carrots, sliced
1 parsnip, thickly sliced
15ml/1 tbsp chopped fresh thyme
2 bay leaves
250ml/8fl oz/1 cup stout
120ml/4fl oz/½ cup Vegetable Stock
5ml/1 tsp yeast extract
5ml/1 tsp soft dark brown sugar
350g/12oz/3 cups drained canned chestnuts, halved
30ml/2 tbsp cornflour (cornstarch), mixed to a paste with 30ml/2 tbsp cold water
150g/5oz Stilton cheese, cubed
beaten egg, to glaze
salt and ground black pepper

For the pastry

115g/4oz/1 cup wholemeal (whole wheat) flour
a pinch of salt
50g/2oz/¼ cup butter
15ml/1 tbsp chopped fresh thyme

1 Make the pastry. Put the flour and salt in a bowl. Rub in the butter until the mixture resembles fine breadcrumbs. Add the thyme and enough water to form a soft dough. Knead it lightly, wrap and chill for 30 minutes.

2 Make the filling. Heat the oil in a pan and cook the onions until softened. Add the mushrooms and cook for 3 minutes. Stir in the carrots, parsnip and herbs. Cover and cook for 3 minutes.

3 Pour in the stout and stock, then stir in the yeast extract and sugar. Simmer, covered, for 5 minutes. Add the chestnuts and season to taste. Stir in the cornflour paste until the sauce thickens. Stir in the cheese and heat until melted, stirring.

4 Preheat the oven to 220°C/425°F/Gas 7. Spoon the chestnut mixture into a 1.5 litre/2½ pint/6¼ cup pie dish. Roll out the pastry to make a lid. Dampen the edges of the dish and cover with the pastry. Seal, trim and crimp the edges. Cut a small slit in the top of the pie and use any surplus pastry to make pastry leaves. Brush with egg and bake for 30 minutes.

Leek Roulade with Cheese, Walnuts & Peppers

This is surprisingly easy to prepare and makes a good main course.

Serves 4–6

50g/2oz/¼ cup butter, plus extra
   for greasing
30ml/2 tbsp fine dried
   white breadcrumbs
75g/3oz/1 cup freshly grated
   Parmesan cheese
2 leeks, thinly sliced
40g/1½oz/6 tbsp plain (all-
   purpose) flour
250ml/8fl oz/1 cup milk
5ml/1 tsp Dijon mustard
about 2.5ml/½ tsp freshly
   grated nutmeg

2 large (US extra large) eggs,
   separated, plus 1 egg white
2.5ml/½ tsp cream of tartar
salt and ground black pepper

For the filling

2 large red (bell) peppers, halved
   and seeded
350g/12oz/1½ cups
   ricotta cheese
75g/3oz/¾ cup
   walnuts, chopped
4 spring onions (scallions),
   finely chopped
15g/½oz/½ cup fresh
   basil leaves

1 Preheat the oven to 190°C/375°F/Gas 5. Grease a 30 x 23cm/12 x 9in Swiss roll tin (jelly roll pan) and line it with baking parchment. Sprinkle the breadcrumbs and 30ml/2 tbsp of the Parmesan evenly over the paper.

2 Melt the butter in a pan and cook the leeks gently for 5 minutes, until softened but not browned. Stir in the flour and cook for 1 minute, stirring constantly. Add the milk, whisking constantly until the mixture boils and thickens.

3 Stir in the mustard and nutmeg and season to taste. Reserve 30–45ml/2–3 tbsp of the remaining Parmesan, then stir the rest into the sauce. Cool slightly, then beat in the egg yolks.

4 Whisk the egg whites and cream of tartar until stiff. Stir 2–3 spoonfuls of the egg white into the leek mixture to lighten it, then carefully fold in the rest.

5 Pour the mixture into the tin and level the surface. Bake for 15–18 minutes, until risen and just firm.

6 Make the filling. Grill (broil) the peppers, skin-side uppermost, until black and blistered. Place in a bowl, cover with crumpled kitchen paper and leave for 10 minutes. Peel off the skin and cut the peppers into long strips.

7 Beat the cheese with the walnuts and spring onions. Chop half the basil and beat it into the mixture. Season to taste.

8 Sprinkle a large sheet of baking parchment with the remaining Parmesan. Turn out the roulade on to it. Strip off the lining paper and cool slightly. Spread the cheese mixture over and top with the red pepper strips. Tear the remaining basil leaves and sprinkle them over the top. Using the paper as a guide, roll up the roulade and roll it on to a serving platter. Serve warm or leave to cool completely.

Crêpes with Butternut Filling

These melt-in-the-mouth crêpes are wonderful served with a green salad and a rich tomato sauce.

Serves 4

115g/4oz/1 cup plain (all-
   purpose) flour
50g/2oz/scant ½ cup polenta
   or cornmeal
2.5ml/½ tsp mild chilli powder
2 large (US extra large)
   eggs, beaten
about 450ml/¾ pint/scant
   2 cups milk
25g/1oz/2 tbsp butter, melted
vegetable oil, for greasing
salt and ground black pepper

For the filling

45ml/3 tbsp olive oil
450g/1lb/3½ cups seeded and
   diced butternut squash
pinch of dried red chilli flakes
2 large leeks, thickly sliced
2.5ml/½ tsp chopped
   fresh thyme
3 chicory (Belgian endive) heads,
   thickly sliced
115g/4oz goat's cheese, cubed
75g/3oz/¾ cup walnuts,
   coarsely chopped
30ml/2 tbsp chopped fresh
   parsley, plus extra to garnish
45ml/3 tbsp freshly grated
   Parmesan cheese

1 Mix the flour, polenta, chilli powder and a pinch of salt and make a well in the centre. Add the eggs and a little of the milk. Whisk, gradually incorporating the flour mixture and adding enough milk to make a creamy batter. Set aside for 1 hour.

2 Whisk the melted butter into the batter. Heat a lightly greased crêpe pan. Pour in about 60ml/4 tbsp of the batter, cook for 2–3 minutes, turn over and cook for 1–2 minutes, then slide out. Make more crêpes in the same way.

3 Make the filling. Heat 30ml/2 tbsp of the oil in a frying pan and cook the squash, stirring frequently, for 10 minutes. Stir in the chilli flakes, leeks and thyme and cook for 5 minutes. Add the chicory and cook, stirring frequently, for 4–5 minutes. Cool, then stir in the goat's cheese, walnuts and parsley. Season well. Preheat the oven to 200°C/400°F/Gas 6. Lightly grease an ovenproof dish. Stuff each crêpe with 30–45ml/2–3 tbsp of the filling and place in the dish. Sprinkle with the Parmesan and drizzle with the remaining olive oil. Bake for 10–15 minutes.

Baked Herb Crêpes

A spinach, cheese and pine nut filling turns crêpes into party food.

Serves 4

25g/1oz/1 cup chopped fresh herbs
15ml/1 tbsp sunflower oil, plus extra for frying and greasing
120ml/4fl oz/½ cup milk
3 eggs
25g/1oz/¼ cup plain (all-purpose) flour

For the sauce
30ml/2 tbsp olive oil
1 small onion, chopped
2 garlic cloves, crushed
400g/14oz can chopped tomatoes
pinch of soft light brown sugar

For the filling
450g/1lb fresh spinach, cooked and drained
175g/6oz/¾ cup ricotta cheese
25g/1oz pine nuts, toasted
5 pieces of sun-dried tomato in oil, drained and chopped
4 egg whites
30ml/2 tbsp shredded fresh basil
salt and ground black pepper

1 Process the herbs and oil in a food processor until smooth. Add the milk, eggs and flour with a pinch of salt. Process again until smooth. Leave to rest for 30 minutes.

2 Heat a lightly greased crêpe pan. Pour in one-eighth of the batter. Cook for 2 minutes, turn over and cook for 1–2 minutes more. Slide the crêpe out of the pan. Make seven more crêpes.

3 Make the sauce. Heat the oil in a small pan and cook the onion and garlic gently for 5 minutes. Add the tomatoes and sugar and cook for about 10 minutes, until thickened. Purée in a blender or food processor, then sieve into a pan and set aside.

4 Mix all the filling ingredients except the egg whites, seasoning with salt and pepper. Whisk the egg whites until stiff. Stir one-third into the spinach mixture, then fold in the rest.

5 Preheat the oven to 190°C/375°F/Gas 5. Place one crêpe at a time on an oiled baking sheet, add a spoonful of filling and fold into four. Bake for 12 minutes. Reheat the sauce and serve.

Moroccan Crêpes

An unusual and tasty dish which makes a good talking point at the dinner table.

Serves 4–6

15ml/1 tbsp olive oil
1 large onion, chopped
250g/9oz fresh spinach leaves
400g/14oz can chickpeas
2 courgettes (zucchini), grated
30ml/2 tbsp chopped fresh coriander (cilantro)
2 eggs, beaten
salt and ground black pepper
fresh coriander leaves, to garnish

For the crêpes
150g/5oz/1¼ cups plain (all-purpose) flour
1 egg
about 350ml/12fl oz/1½ cups milk
75ml/5 tbsp water
15ml/1 tbsp sunflower oil, plus extra for greasing

For the sauce
25g/1oz/2 tbsp butter
30ml/2 tbsp plain (all-purpose) flour
about 300ml/½ pint/1¼ cups milk

1 Make the batter by blending the flour, egg, milk and water until smooth in a blender. Stir in the oil and a pinch of salt. Heat a lightly greased frying pan and ladle in about one-eighth of the batter. Cook for 2–3 minutes, without turning, then slide the pancake out of the pan. Make seven more pancakes.

2 Heat the olive oil in a small pan and cook the onion until soft. Set aside. Wash the spinach, place it in a pan and cook until wilted, shaking the pan occasionally. Chop the spinach coarsely. Drain the chickpeas, place in a bowl of cold water and rub them until the skins float to the surface. Drain the chickpeas and mash roughly with a fork. Add the onion, courgettes, spinach and coriander. Stir in the eggs, season and mix well.

3 Preheat the oven to 180°C/350°F/Gas 4. Place the pancakes, cooked side up, on a board and spoon the filling down the centres. Roll up and place in an oiled ovenproof dish. Make the sauce. Melt the butter in a pan, stir in the flour and cook for 1 minute. Gradually whisk in the milk until the mixture boils. Season and pour over the pancakes. Bake for 15 minutes, until golden. Serve garnished with the coriander leaves.

Gnocchi with Gorgonzola Sauce

A simple potato dough is used to make these ridged dumplings, which are delicious with a creamy cheese sauce.

Serves 4

450g/1lb potatoes, unpeeled
1 large (US extra large) egg
about 115g/4oz/1 cup plain (all-
  purpose) flour

salt and ground black pepper
fresh thyme sprigs, to garnish
60ml/4 tbsp freshly shaved
  Parmesan cheese, to serve

For the sauce

115g/4oz Gorgonzola cheese
60ml/4 tbsp double
  (heavy) cream
15ml/1 tbsp chopped fresh thyme

1 Put the potatoes in a pan of cold water. Bring to the boil, add salt and cook the potatoes for about 20 minutes, until tender. Drain and, when cool enough to handle, remove the skins.

2 Tip the potatoes into a sieve placed over a mixing bowl. Press through with the back of a spoon. Season, then beat in the egg. Add the flour, a little at a time, stirring after each addition until you have a smooth dough. (You may not need all the flour.) Knead the dough on a floured surface for 3 minutes, adding more flour if necessary, until smooth, soft and no longer sticky.

3 Divide the dough into six equal pieces. Gently roll each piece between floured hands into a 2.5cm/1in wide log shape that is 15cm/6in long. Cut each log into six equal pieces, then gently roll each piece in the flour. Form into gnocchi by gently pressing each piece with the tines of a fork to leave ridges in the dough.

4 Bring a large pan of water to the boil. Drop in the gnocchi, about 12 at a time. After about 2 minutes, they will rise to the surface. Cook for 4–5 minutes more, then lift out with a slotted spoon. Drain and keep hot while you cook the rest.

5 Make the sauce. Place the Gorgonzola, cream and thyme in a large frying pan and heat gently until the cheese melts to a thick, creamy consistency. Add the drained gnocchi and toss well to combine. Garnish with thyme and serve with Parmesan.

Semolina & Pesto Gnocchi

These gnocchi are cooked rounds of semolina paste, which are brushed with melted butter, topped with cheese and baked. They taste wonderful with a home-made tomato sauce.

Serves 4–6

750ml/1¼ pints/3 cups milk
200g/7oz/1¼ cups semolina
45ml/3 tbsp pesto sauce

60ml/4 tbsp finely chopped
  sun-dried tomatoes, patted
  dry if oily
50g/2oz/¼ cup butter, plus extra
  for greasing
75g/3oz/1 cup freshly grated
  Pecorino cheese
2 eggs, beaten
freshly grated nutmeg
salt and ground black pepper
fresh basil sprigs, to garnish
Tomato Sauce, to serve

1 Heat the milk in a large non-stick pan. When it is on the point of boiling, sprinkle in the semolina, stirring constantly until the mixture is smooth and very thick. Lower the heat and simmer for 2 minutes.

2 Remove the pan from the heat and stir in the pesto and sun-dried tomatoes, with half the butter and half the Pecorino. Beat in the eggs, with nutmeg, salt and pepper to taste. Spoon into a clean shallow ovenproof dish to a depth of 1cm/½in and level the surface. Leave to cool, then chill.

3 Preheat the oven to 190°C/375°F/Gas 5. Lightly grease a shallow ovenproof dish. Using a 4cm/1½in round cutter, stamp out as many rounds as possible from the semolina paste.

4 Place the leftover semolina paste on the base of the greased dish and arrange the rounds on top in overlapping circles. Melt the remaining butter and brush it over the gnocchi. Sprinkle over the remaining Pecorino. Bake for 30–40 minutes, until golden. Garnish with the basil and serve with the tomato sauce.

Variation
Use Parmesan instead of Pecorino, if you like.

New Potato, Rosemary & Garlic Pizza

New potatoes, smoked mozzarella, rosemary and garlic make the flavour of this pizza unique.

Serves 2–3
350g/12oz new potatoes
45ml/3 tbsp olive oil
2 garlic cloves, crushed
1 pizza base, 25–30cm/10–12in
  in diameter
1 red onion, very thinly sliced
150g/5oz/1¼ cups grated
  smoked mozzarella cheese
10ml/2 tsp chopped
  fresh rosemary
salt and ground black pepper
30ml/2 tbsp freshly grated
  Parmesan cheese, to garnish

1 Preheat the oven to 220°C/425°F/Gas 7. Bring a large pan of lightly salted water to the boil and cook the potatoes for 5 minutes. Drain well. When cool, peel the potatoes and slice them thinly.

2 Heat 30ml/2 tbsp of the oil in a frying pan. Add the sliced potatoes and garlic and cook over a medium heat, stirring occasionally, for 5–8 minutes until tender.

3 Brush the pizza base with the remaining oil. Sprinkle over the onion, then arrange the potatoes on top.

4 Sprinkle over the mozzarella and rosemary. Grind over plenty of black pepper. Bake for 15–20 minutes, until the crust is crisp and golden. Sprinkle over the grated Parmesan and serve.

> **Cook's Tips**
> • It's easy to overestimate how many new potatoes you need to cook for a family meal. Next time you find yourself with leftovers, use them to make this tasty pizza.
> • Smoked mozzarella, also known as mozzarella affumicata, is available from supermarkets and delicatessens.

Quattro Formaggi Pizzas

As the Italian title suggests, these tasty little pizzas are topped with four different types of cheese and have a very rich flavour.

Serves 4
1 quantity Basic Pizza Dough
flour, for dusting
15ml/1 tbsp olive oil
1 small red onion, very
  thinly sliced
50g/2oz Dolcelatte cheese
50g/2oz mozzarella cheese
50g/2oz Gruyère cheese
30ml/2 tbsp freshly grated
  Parmesan cheese
15ml/1 tbsp chopped fresh thyme
ground black pepper

1 Preheat the oven to 220°C/425°F/Gas 7. Divide the dough into four pieces and roll out each one on a lightly floured surface into a 13cm/5in round.

2 Place well apart on two greased baking sheets, then push up the dough edges to make a thin rim.

3 Heat the olive oil in a small frying pan. Add the red onion slices and cook over a low heat, stirring occasionally for 4–5 minutes, until softened. Divide them among the pizza bases, then brush over any oil remaining in the pan.

4 Cut the Dolcelatte and mozzarella into cubes and sprinkle them over the pizza bases. Grate the Gruyère cheese into a bowl. Add the Parmesan and thyme and mix thoroughly. Sprinkle the mixture over the bases.

5 Grind over plenty of black pepper. Bake for 15–20 minutes, until the crust on each pizza is crisp and golden and the cheese is bubbling. Serve immediately.

> **Variation**
> There's no need to stick slavishly to the suggested cheeses. Any variety that melts readily can be used, but a mixture of soft and hard cheeses gives the best result.

Saffron Risotto

This classic risotto makes a delicious first course or light supper dish.

Serves 4

about 1.2 litres/2 pints/5 cups
   Vegetable Stock
good pinch of saffron threads

75g/3oz/6 tbsp butter
1 onion, finely chopped
275g/10oz/1½ cups risotto rice
75g/3oz/1 cup freshly grated
   Parmesan cheese
salt and ground black pepper
freshly ground black pepper,
   to garnish

1 Bring the stock to the boil in a large pan, then lower the heat so that it barely simmers. Ladle a little stock into a small bowl. Add the saffron threads and leave to infuse (steep).

2 Melt 50g/2oz/4 tbsp of the butter in a large pan. Add the onion and cook over a low heat, stirring frequently, for 3 minutes, until softened.

3 Add the rice. Stir until coated, then add a few ladlefuls of the stock, with the saffron liquid and salt and pepper to taste. Stir over a low heat until the stock has been absorbed.

4 Add the remaining stock in the same way, allowing the rice to absorb all the liquid before adding more, and stirring constantly. After 20–25 minutes, the rice should be *al dente* and the risotto golden yellow, moist and creamy.

5 Gently stir in about two-thirds of the grated Parmesan and the remaining butter. Cover the pan and leave the risotto to stand for 2–3 minutes. Spoon it into a warmed serving bowl and serve immediately, with the remaining grated Parmesan sprinkled on top and some freshly ground black pepper.

Cook's Tip
Risotto rice, such as arborio, has rounder grains than long grain rice and is able to absorb large quantities of liquid, giving the dish its characteristic creamy texture.

Risotto with Summer Vegetables

This is one of the prettiest risottos, especially if you can get yellow courgettes.

Serves 4

150g/5oz/1¼ cups shelled
   fresh peas
115g/4oz/1 cup green beans, cut
   into short lengths
30ml/2 tbsp olive oil
75g/3oz/6 tbsp butter
2 small yellow courgettes
   (zucchini), cut into batons

1 onion, finely chopped
275g/10oz/1½ cups risotto rice
120ml/4fl oz/ ½ cup Italian dry
   white vermouth
about 1 litre/1¾ pints/4 cups
   simmering Vegetable Stock
75g/3oz/1 cup freshly grated
   Parmesan cheese
a small handful of fresh basil
   leaves, finely shredded, plus a
   few whole leaves, to garnish
salt and ground black pepper

1 Bring a large pan of lightly salted water to the boil and blanch the peas and beans for 2–3 minutes, until just tender. Drain, refresh under cold running water, drain again and set aside.

2 Heat the oil and 25g/1oz/2 tbsp of the butter in a medium pan. Add the courgettes and cook over a low heat for about 3 minutes. Remove with a slotted spoon and set aside.

3 Add the onion to the pan and cook, stirring occasionally, for about 3 minutes, until softened.

4 Stir in the rice until coated, then add the vermouth. When most of it has been absorbed, add a few ladlefuls of the stock and season with salt and pepper to taste. Stir over a low heat until the stock has been absorbed.

5 Continue adding the stock, a little at a time, and stirring constantly for about 20 minutes, until all the stock has been added and the risotto is moist and creamy.

6 Gently stir in the vegetables, the remaining butter and about half the grated Parmesan. Heat through, then stir in the shredded basil. Serve immediately, garnished with a few whole basil leaves. Offer the remaining grated Parmesan separately.

Festive Lentil & Nut Loaf

For a special celebration, serve this with all the trimmings, including a vegetarian gravy. Garnish it with fresh cranberries and flat leaf parsley for a really festive effect.

Serves 6–8

115g/4oz/ ½ cup red lentils
115g/4oz/1 cup hazelnuts
115g/4oz/1 cup walnuts
1 large carrot
2 celery sticks
1 large onion
115g/4oz/1⅔ cups mushrooms
50g/2oz/ ¼ cup butter, plus extra
    for greasing
10ml/2 tsp mild curry powder
30ml/2 tbsp tomato ketchup
30ml/2 tbsp vegetarian
    Worcestershire sauce
1 egg, beaten
10ml/2 tsp salt
60ml/4 tbsp chopped
    fresh parsley
150ml/ ¼ pint/ ⅔ cup water

1 Put the lentils in a bowl and add sufficient cold water to cover. Set aside for 1 hour to soak. Grind the nuts in a food processor until quite fine, but not too smooth. Tip the nuts into a large bowl. Coarsely chop the carrot, celery, onion and mushrooms, add them to the food processor and process until finely chopped.

2 Heat the butter in a pan. Add the vegetables and cook gently over a low heat, stirring occasionally, for 5 minutes. Stir in the curry powder and cook for 1 minute more. Remove from the heat and set aside to cool.

3 Drain the soaked lentils and stir them into the ground nuts. Add the vegetables, ketchup, vegetarian Worcestershire sauce, egg, salt, parsley and water.

4 Preheat the oven to 190°C/375°F/Gas 5. Grease a 1kg/2¼lb loaf tin (pan) and line with greaseproof (waxed) paper or a sheet of foil. Press the mixture into the tin.

5 Bake for 1–1¼ hours, until just firm, covering the top with foil if it starts to burn. Leave to stand for 15 minutes before you turn it out and peel off the paper. It will be fairly soft when cut.

Mushroom & Mixed Nut Roast

The seed topping on this roast, visible when you turn it out, looks very attractive and is a good contrast to the tender loaf.

Serves 4

30ml/2 tbsp sunflower oil, plus
    extra for greasing
45ml/3 tbsp sunflower seeds
45ml/3 tbsp sesame seeds
1 onion, coarsely chopped
2 celery sticks, coarsely chopped
1 green (bell) pepper, seeded
    and chopped
225g/8oz/3¼ cups mixed
    mushrooms, chopped
1 garlic clove, crushed
115g/4oz/2 cups fresh wholemeal
    (whole-wheat) breadcrumbs
115g/4oz/1 cup chopped
    mixed nuts
50g/2oz/ ⅓ cup sultanas
    (golden raisins)
small piece of fresh root ginger,
    finely chopped
10ml/2 tsp coriander
    seeds, crushed
30ml/2 tbsp light soy sauce
1 egg, beaten
salt and ground black pepper
celery and coriander (cilantro)
    leaves, to garnish
Tomato Sauce, to serve

1 Brush a 675g/1½lb loaf tin (pan) with sunflower oil and line with greaseproof (waxed) paper. Sprinkle the sunflower and sesame seeds evenly over the base.

2 Preheat the oven to 190°C/375°F/Gas 5. Heat the oil in a large frying pan. Add the onion, celery, green pepper, mixed mushrooms and garlic and cook over a low heat, stirring occasionally, for about 5 minutes, until the onion has softened but not coloured. Remove the pan from the heat and set aside.

3 Mix together the breadcrumbs and nuts in a large bowl. Tip in the contents of the frying pan, then stir in the sultanas, ginger, coriander seeds and soy sauce. Bind with the egg, then season to taste with salt and pepper.

4 Press the mixture evenly into the prepared tin and bake for 45 minutes. Loosen the sides of the loaf with a knife, then leave it to cool for 2–3 minutes. Turn out on to a serving dish and garnish with the celery and coriander leaves. Serve immediately with the tomato sauce.

SIDE DISHES, SALADS & BREAD

The right accompaniments to the main course, whether fragrant rice, a refreshing salad or crusty, home-made bread, are what completes it. Mix and match these recipes with different main dishes to create truly sensational meals. You don't have to spend a lot of extra time for fabulous results either. Garlic Sweet Potato Mash takes no longer than plain potatoes and simply melts in the mouth. For the summer, Radish, Mango & Apple Salad is deliciously different as well as being simple to make, and why not complement a festive nut roast with succulent Caramelized Shallots?

Making your own bread is more time-consuming, but a freshly baked loaf is a real treat. In any case, most of the time required is to allow the dough to rise, so you can set it aside and get on with preparing the rest of the meal or even put your feet up with a glass of wine. Serve fresh rustic bread with soup and, perhaps, cheese for a tasty lunch or make a mouth-watering focaccia to accompany pasta or risotto. Even Indian naan bread can be baked at home, without a traditional clay oven, with stunning results.

Baked Fennel with a Crumb Crust

The delicate aniseed flavour of baked fennel makes it a very good accompaniment to pasta dishes and risottos.

Serves 4
3 fennel bulbs, cut lengthways
  into quarters
30ml/2 tbsp olive oil
50g/2oz/1 cup day-old wholemeal
  (whole-wheat) breadcrumbs
1 garlic clove, chopped
30ml/2 tbsp chopped fresh
  flat leaf parsley
salt and ground black pepper
fennel leaves, to garnish

1 Bring a pan of lightly salted water to the boil over a medium heat. Add the fennel quarters, bring back to the boil, then lower the heat and simmer gently for about 10 minutes, or until they are just tender.

2 Preheat the oven to 190°C/375°F/Gas 5. Drain the fennel and place the pieces in an ovenproof dish or roasting pan. Brush with half the olive oil.

3 Put the breadcrumbs, garlic and parsley in a separate bowl and drizzle over the remaining olive oil. Season to taste with salt and pepper. Mix lightly, then sprinkle the mixture evenly over the fennel.

4 Bake for 30 minutes, or until the fennel is tender and the breadcrumbs are crisp and golden. Serve hot, garnished with feathery fennel leaves.

Variations
• Add 60ml/4 tbsp finely grated, strongly flavoured cheese, such as mature (sharp) Cheddar, Red Leicester or Parmesan, to the breadcrumb topping.
• Add two or three cored and sliced red eating apples to the dish with the cooked fennel quarters.

Spinach with Raisins & Pine Nuts

Wilted spinach benefits from a touch of sweetness, as this delicious Spanish dish amply illustrates.

Serves 4
50g/2oz/1/3 cup raisins
1 thick slice crusty white bread
45ml/3 tbsp olive oil
25g/1oz/1/4 cup pine nuts
500g/1 1/4lb young spinach leaves,
  stalks removed
2 garlic cloves, crushed
salt and ground black pepper

1 Put the raisins in a small bowl. Cover with boiling water and leave to soak for 10 minutes.

2 Cut off the crusts from the bread and discard. Cut the bread into small cubes.

3 Heat 30ml/2 tbsp of the oil in a large, heavy frying pan. Add the bread cubes and fry over a medium heat, stirring and turning frequently, until golden all over. Lift out with a slotted spoon and drain well on kitchen paper.

4 Add the remaining oil to the pan. When it is hot, fry the pine nuts until beginning to colour. Add the spinach and garlic and cook quickly, turning the spinach until it has just wilted.

5 Drain the raisins, toss them into the pan and season lightly with salt and pepper. Transfer to a warmed serving dish. Sprinkle with the croûtons and serve immediately.

Variation
Swiss chard or spinach beet can be used instead of the spinach, but will need to be cooked a little more.

Courgettes in Rich Tomato Sauce

Serve this colourful dish hot or cold. Cut the courgettes fairly thickly, so they stay slightly crunchy.

Serves 4
15ml/1 tbsp olive oil
1 onion, chopped
1 garlic clove, chopped
4 courgettes (zucchini), sliced

400g/14oz can chopped
  tomatoes, drained
2 tomatoes, peeled, seeded
  and chopped
5ml/1 tsp vegetable
  bouillon powder
15ml/1 tbsp tomato
  purée (paste)
salt and ground black pepper

1 Heat the oil in a heavy pan and sauté the onion and garlic until softened, stirring occasionally. Add the courgettes and cook for 5 minutes more.
2 Tip in the canned and fresh tomatoes, then stir in the bouillon powder and tomato purée. Simmer for 10–15 minutes, until the sauce has thickened and the courgettes are just tender. Season to taste with salt and pepper and serve.

Braised Leeks with Carrots

Sweet carrots and leeks go
well together, especially
when married with a little
chopped mint, chervil or flat
leaf parsley.

Serves 6
65g/2¹/₂oz/5 tbsp butter
675g/1¹/₂lb carrots, thickly sliced
2 bay leaves
2.5ml/ ¹/₂ tsp caster
　(superfine) sugar
75ml/5 tbsp water
675g/1¹/₂lb leeks, cut into
　5cm/2in lengths
120ml/4fl oz/ ¹/₂ cup white wine
30ml/2 tbsp chopped fresh mint
salt and ground black pepper

1 Melt 25g/1oz/2 tbsp of the butter in a pan and cook the
carrots gently for 4–5 minutes. Do not let them brown.

2 Add the bay leaves, caster sugar and water. Season with salt
and pepper to taste. Bring to the boil, cover tightly and cook for
10–15 minutes, or until the carrots are tender, shaking the pan
frequently to stop the carrots from sticking. Remove the lid,
then boil until the juices have evaporated, leaving the carrots
moist and glazed.

3 Meanwhile, melt 25g/1oz/2 tbsp of the remaining butter in a
pan that is wide enough to hold the leeks in a single layer. Add
the leeks, stir to coat them in butter, then cook over a low heat
for 4–5 minutes, without letting them brown.

4 Stir in the wine and half the mint, then season to taste. Heat
until simmering, then cover and cook gently for 5–8 minutes,
or until the leeks are tender, but have not collapsed.

5 Uncover the leeks and turn them in the buttery juices.
Increase the heat, then boil the liquid rapidly until reduced to a
few tablespoons.

6 Add the carrots to the leeks and reheat them gently, then
swirl in the remaining butter. Adjust the seasoning, if necessary.
Transfer to a warmed serving dish and serve sprinkled with the
remaining mint.

Caramelized Shallots

Wonderful with well-
flavoured nut roasts or lentil
loaves, these also taste good
with other braised or
roasted vegetables, such as
chunks of butternut squash.

Serves 4–6
50g/2oz/ ¹/₄ cup butter
500g/1¹/₄lb shallots or small
　onions, peeled, with root
　ends intact
15ml/1 tbsp golden caster
　(superfine) sugar
30ml/2 tbsp red or white wine
150ml/ ¹/₄ pint/ ²/₃ cup
　Vegetable Stock
2–3 fresh bay leaves
salt and ground black pepper
fresh thyme sprigs, to garnish

1 Melt the butter in a large frying pan and add the shallots or
onions in a single layer. Cook over a low heat, turning
occasionally, for about 10 minutes, until lightly browned.

2 Sprinkle the sugar over the shallots or onions and cook
gently, turning them in the juices, until the sugar begins to
caramelize. Add the wine and cook for 4–5 minutes.

3 Pour in the stock and add the bay leaves. Season with salt
and pepper to taste. Cover and cook for 5 minutes, then
remove the lid and cook until the liquid evaporates and the
shallots are tender and glazed.

4 Adjust the seasoning, if necessary, and spoon into a serving
bowl. Garnish with the sprigs of thyme and serve.

> **Variation**
> *Shallots with Chestnuts: Cook the shallots as above, but toss in
> 250g/9oz/2–3 cups partially cooked chestnuts just before
> adding the stock. Cook the two vegetables together for about
> 5–10 minutes, then serve sprinkled with plenty of chopped
> flat leaf parsley.*

Oven Chip Roasties

These oven roasties taste just as good as the deep-fried version and are much easier to cook. They also make very popular canapés to serve with pre-dinner drinks.

Serves 4–6
150ml/ ¼ pint/ ⅔ cup olive oil
4 medium to large baking potatoes
5ml/1 tsp mixed dried herbs (optional)
sea salt flakes
mayonnaise, to serve

1 Preheat the oven to the highest temperature; this is generally 240°C/475°F/Gas 9. Lightly oil a large shallow roasting pan and place it in the oven to get really hot while you are preparing the potatoes.

2 Cut the potatoes in half lengthways, then into long thin wedges, or thicker ones if you like. Brush each side lightly with olive oil.

3 When the oven is really hot, remove the roasting pan carefully and sprinkle the potato wedges over it, spreading them out in a single layer over the hot oil.

4 Sprinkle the potato wedges with the herbs and sea salt flakes and then roast for about 20 minutes, or longer if they are thicker, turning once so that they brown evenly, until they are golden brown, crisp and lightly puffy. Remove from the oven, drain thoroughly on kitchen paper and serve with a spoonful of mayonnaise.

Variations
• *Sweet potatoes also make fine oven chips (fries). Prepare and roast as for regular potatoes, although you may find they do not take so long to cook.*
• *You can flavour the roasties with mild paprika instead of mixed herbs.*
• *Serve with lemon juice instead of mayonnaise.*

Garlic Sweet Potato Mash

Orange-fleshed sweet potatoes not only look good; they taste delicious mashed with garlic butter.

Serves 4
900g/2lb sweet potatoes
45ml/3 tbsp butter
3 garlic cloves, crushed
salt and ground black pepper

1 Bring a large pan of lightly salted water to the boil. Add the sweet potatoes and cook for about 15 minutes, or until tender. Drain very well, return to the pan and cover tightly.

2 Melt the butter in a frying pan and sauté the garlic over a low heat, stirring constantly, for 1–2 minutes, until light golden.

3 Pour the garlic butter over the potatoes, season with salt and pepper, and mash until smooth and creamy. Serve immediately.

Perfect Creamed Potatoes

Smooth mashed potatoes taste very good and are the ideal accompaniment for other vegetarian dishes.

about 150ml/¼ pint/⅔ cup hot milk
freshly grated nutmeg
a few fresh basil leaves or parsley sprigs, chopped
salt and ground black pepper
fresh basil leaves, to garnish

Serves 4
900g/2lb firm but not waxy potatoes, diced
45ml/3 tbsp extra virgin olive oil

1 Put the potatoes in a pan of cold water and bring to the boil. Cook until just tender. Drain very well. Press the potatoes through a potato ricer or mash with a potato masher.
2 Beat in the olive oil and enough hot milk to give a smooth, thick purée.
3 Flavour to taste with the nutmeg and seasoning, then stir in the chopped fresh herbs. Spoon into a warm serving dish and serve immediately, garnished with the basil leaves.

Potato Latkes

These traditional Jewish potato pancakes taste wonderful with apple sauce and sour cream.

Serves 4
2 medium floury potatoes
1 onion
1 large (US extra large)
   egg, beaten
30ml/2 tbsp medium-ground
   matzo meal
vegetable oil, for frying
salt and ground black pepper

1 Peel the potatoes and grate them coarsely. Grate the onion in the same way. Mix the potatoes and onion in a large colander in the sink, but do not rinse them. Press them down, squeezing out as much of the thick starchy liquid as possible. Tip the potato mixture into a large bowl.

2 Immediately stir in the beaten egg. Add the matzo meal, stirring gently to mix. Season with salt and plenty of pepper.

3 Preheat the oven to 150°C/300°F/Gas 2. Pour oil to a depth of 1cm/½in into a heavy frying pan. Heat until a small piece of day-old bread, added to the oil, sizzles. Take a spoonful of the potato mixture and lower it carefully into the oil. Continue adding spoonfuls, leaving space between each one.

4 Flatten the pancakes slightly with the back of a spoon. Fry for a few minutes until golden brown on the underside, then turn them over and continue frying until golden brown all over.

5 Drain the latkes on kitchen paper, then transfer to an ovenproof serving dish and keep warm in the oven while frying the remainder. Serve hot.

> **Variation**
> Try using equal quantities of potatoes and Jerusalem artichokes for a really distinct flavour.

New Potatoes with Shallot Butter

New potatoes are always a treat and are superb with this delicate butter.

Serves 6
500g/1¼lb small new potatoes
25g/1oz/2 tbsp butter

3 shallots, finely chopped
2 garlic cloves, crushed
5ml/1 tsp chopped fresh tarragon
5ml/1 tsp chopped fresh chives
5ml/1 tsp chopped fresh parsley
salt and ground black pepper

1 Bring a pan of lightly salted water to the boil. Add the potatoes and cook for 15–20 minutes, until just tender. Drain them well.

2 Melt the butter in a large frying pan. Cook the shallots and garlic over a low heat, stirring occasionally, for 5 minutes. Add the potatoes to the pan and mix with the shallot butter. Season to taste with salt and pepper. Cook, stirring constantly, until the potatoes are heated through.

3 Transfer the potatoes to a warmed serving bowl. Sprinkle with the chopped herbs and serve immediately.

New Potatoes with Sour Cream

This is a traditional Russian way of serving potatoes. The sour cream may be flavoured with spring onions, as here, or chopped fresh chives.

Serves 6
900g/2lb new potatoes
150ml/¼ pint/⅔ cup sour cream
4 spring onions (scallions),
   thinly sliced
salt and ground black pepper
15ml/1 tbsp chopped fresh dill,
   to garnish

1 Bring a pan of lightly salted water to the boil. Add the potatoes and cook for 15–20 minutes, until just tender. Drain.
2 Mix the sour cream and spring onions and season to taste with salt and pepper. Place the potatoes in a warm serving dish, add the cream mixture and toss lightly. Garnish with dill.

Pilau Rice with Whole Spices

This fragrant rice dish makes a perfect accompaniment to any Indian vegetarian dish.

Serves 4
600ml/1 pint/2½ cups hot
   Vegetable Stock
generous pinch of saffron threads
250g/9oz/1⅓ cups basmati rice
50g/2oz/¼ cup butter
1 onion, chopped
1 garlic clove, crushed
½ cinnamon stick
6 green cardamom pods
1 bay leaf
50g/2oz/⅓ cup sultanas
   (golden raisins)
15ml/1 tbsp sunflower oil
50g/2oz/½ cup cashew nuts
naan bread and tomato and
   onion salad, to serve (optional)

1 Pour the stock into a jug (pitcher) and stir in the saffron threads. Set aside to infuse (steep). Rinse the rice several times in cold water. If there is time, leave it to soak for 30 minutes in the water used for the final rinse.

2 Heat the butter in a pan and cook the onion and garlic for 5 minutes. Stir in the cinnamon stick, cardamoms and bay leaf and cook for 2 minutes.

3 Drain the rice thoroughly, add it to the pan and cook, stirring, for 2 minutes more. Pour in the saffron-flavoured stock and add the sultanas. Bring to the boil, stir, then lower the heat, cover and cook gently for about 10 minutes, or until the rice is tender and all the liquid has been absorbed.

4 Meanwhile, heat the oil in a frying pan and fry the cashew nuts until browned. Drain well on kitchen paper. Sprinkle the cashew nuts over the rice. Serve with naan bread and a tomato and onion salad, if you like.

> **Cook's Tip**
> Don't be tempted to use black cardamoms in this dish. They are coarser and more strongly flavoured than green cardamoms and are used only in dishes that are cooked for a long time.

Indonesian Coconut Rice

This way of cooking rice is very popular throughout the whole of South-east Asia.

Serves 4–6
350g/12oz/1¾ cups Thai
   fragrant rice
400ml/14fl oz can coconut milk
300ml/½ pint/1¼ cups water
2.5ml/½ tsp ground coriander
5cm/2in piece of cinnamon stick
1 lemon grass stalk, bruised
1 bay leaf
salt
deep-fried onions (see Cook's Tip),
   to garnish

1 Put the rice in a strainer and rinse thoroughly under cold water. Drain well, then put in a pan. Pour in the coconut milk and water. Add the coriander, cinnamon stick, lemon grass and bay leaf. Season with salt. Bring to the boil, then lower the heat, cover and simmer for 8–10 minutes.

2 Lift the lid and check that all the liquid has been absorbed, then fork the rice through carefully, removing the cinnamon stick, lemon grass and bay leaf.

3 Cover the pan with a tight-fitting lid and continue to cook over the lowest possible heat for 3–5 minutes more.

4 Pile the rice on to a warm serving dish and serve garnished with the crisp, deep-fried onions.

> **Cook's Tips**
> • Deep-fried onions are a traditional Indonesian garnish. You can buy them ready-prepared from Asian food stores, but they are easy to make at home. Slice 450g/1lb onions very thinly, then spread the slices in a single layer on kitchen paper. Leave to dry for at least 1 hour, preferably longer. Deep-fry in batches in hot oil until crisp and golden. Drain on kitchen paper and use immediately, or cool, then store in an airtight container.
> • If you have access to a well-stocked Asian supermarket, substitute a pandan leaf for the bay leaf. Pull the tines of a fork through the leaf to release its flavour.

Fattoush

This simple salad has been served for centuries in the Middle East. It has been adopted by restaurateurs all over the world, and you are as likely to encounter it in San Francisco as in Syria.

Serves 4

1 yellow or red (bell) pepper, seeded and sliced
1 large cucumber, coarsely chopped
4–5 tomatoes, chopped
1 bunch spring onions (scallions), sliced
30ml/2 tbsp finely chopped fresh parsley
30ml/2 tbsp finely chopped fresh mint
30ml/2 tbsp finely chopped fresh coriander (cilantro)
2 garlic cloves, crushed
juice of 1 ½ lemons
45ml/3 tbsp olive oil
salt and ground black pepper
2 pitta breads, to serve

1 Place the yellow or red pepper, cucumber and tomatoes in a salad bowl. Add the spring onions and chopped herbs.

2 Make the dressing. Mix the garlic with the lemon juice in a jug (pitcher). Gradually whisk in the olive oil, then season to taste with salt and pepper. Pour the dressing over the salad and toss lightly to mix.

3 Toast the pitta bread, in a toaster or under a hot grill (broiler) until crisp. Serve with the salad.

Cook's Tip
People either love or hate fresh coriander (cilantro). If you hate it, omit it and double the quantity of parsley.

Variation
If you prefer, make this salad in the traditional way. After toasting the pitta breads until crisp, crush them in your hand and sprinkle them over the salad before serving.

Radish, Mango & Apple Salad

Clean, crisp tastes and mellow flavours make this salad a good choice at any time, although it is at its best with fresh garden radishes in early summer.

Serves 4

10–15 radishes
1 eating apple
2 celery sticks, thinly sliced
1 small ripe mango
fresh dill sprigs, to garnish

For the dressing
120ml/4fl oz/ ½ cup low-fat crème fraîche
10ml/2 tsp creamed horseradish
15ml/1 tbsp chopped fresh dill
salt and ground black pepper

1 Make the dressing by mixing the crème fraîche with the creamed horseradish and dill in a small jug (pitcher). Season with a little salt and pepper.

2 Trim the radishes, then slice them thinly. Place them in a bowl. Cut the unpeeled apple into quarters, remove the core from each wedge, then slice them thinly and add it to the bowl with the sliced celery.

3 Cut through the mango lengthways either side of the stone (pit). Leaving the skin on each section, cross hatch the flesh, then bend it back so that the cubes stand proud of the skin. Slice them off with a small knife and add them to the bowl.

4 Pour the dressing over the vegetables and fruit and stir gently to coat. When ready to serve, spoon the salad into a salad bowl and garnish with the dill.

Cook's Tip
Radishes are members of the mustard family and may be red or white, round or elongated. They vary considerably in their strength of flavour; small, slender French radishes are especially mild and sweet. Whatever type you are buying, look for small, firm, brightly coloured specimens, with no sign of limpness.

Feta & Mint Potato Salad

The oddly named pink fir apple potatoes are perfect for this salad, and taste great with feta cheese, yogurt and fresh mint.

Serves 4
500g/1¼lb pink fir
   apple potatoes
90g/3½oz feta cheese, crumbled

For the dressing
225g/8oz/1 cup natural
   (plain) yogurt
15g/½oz/ ½ cup fresh
   mint leaves
30ml/2 tbsp mayonnaise
salt and ground black pepper

1 Steam the potatoes over a pan of boiling water for about 20 minutes, until tender.

2 Meanwhile, make the dressing. Mix the yogurt and mint in a food processor and pulse until the mint leaves are finely chopped. Scrape the mixture into a small bowl, stir in the mayonnaise and season to taste with salt and pepper.

3 Drain the potatoes well and tip them into a large bowl. Spoon the dressing over and sprinkle the feta cheese on top. Serve immediately.

> **Cook's Tip**
> Pink fir apple potatoes have a smooth waxy texture and retain their shape when cooked, making them ideal for salads. Charlotte, Belle de Fontenay and other special salad potatoes could be used instead.

> **Variations**
> • Crumbled Kefalotiri or young Manchego could be used instead of the feta.
> • For a richer dressing, use Greek (US strained plain) yogurt or sour cream.

Baked Sweet Potato Salad

This salad has a truly tropical taste and is ideal served with Asian or Caribbean dishes.

Serves 4–6
1kg/2¼lb sweet potatoes
1 red (bell) pepper, seeded and
   finely diced
3 celery sticks, finely diced
¼ red onion,
   finely chopped
1 fresh red chilli, finely chopped
salt and ground black pepper
coriander (cilantro) leaves,
   to garnish

For the dressing
45ml/3 tbsp chopped fresh
   coriander (cilantro)
juice of 1 lime
150ml/ ¼ pint/ ⅔ cup natural
   (plain) yogurt

1 Preheat the oven to 200°C/400°F/Gas 6. Wash the potatoes, pierce them all over with a fork and bake for about 40 minutes, or until tender.

2 Meanwhile, make the dressing. Whisk together the coriander, lime juice and yogurt in a small bowl and season to taste with salt and pepper. Chill in the refrigerator while you prepare the remaining salad ingredients.

3 In a large bowl, mix the diced red pepper, celery, chopped onion and chilli together.

4 Remove the potatoes from the oven. As soon as they are cool enough to handle, peel them and cut them into cubes. Add them to the bowl. Drizzle the dressing over and toss carefully. Taste and adjust the seasoning, if necessary. Serve, garnished with coriander leaves.

> **Cook's Tip**
> It is generally thought that the seeds are the hottest part of a chilli. In fact, they contain no capsaicin – the hot element – but it is intensely concentrated in the flesh surrounding them. Removing the seeds usually removes this extra hot flesh.

Fragrant Lentil & Spinach Salad

This earthy salad is great for a picnic or barbecue.

Serves 6
225g/8oz/1 cup Puy lentils
1 fresh bay leaf
1 celery stick
1 fresh thyme sprig
30ml/2 tbsp olive oil
1 onion, thinly sliced
10ml/2 tsp crushed toasted
   cumin seeds
400g/14oz young spinach leaves
30–45ml/2–3 tbsp chopped fresh
   parsley, plus a few extra sprigs
   for garnishing

salt and ground black pepper
toasted French bread, to serve

For the dressing
45ml/3 tbsp extra virgin olive oil
5ml/1 tsp Dijon mustard
15–25ml/3–5 tsp red
   wine vinegar
1 small garlic clove,
   finely chopped
2.5ml/½ tsp finely grated
   lemon rind

1 Rinse the lentils and place them in a large pan. Add water to cover. Tie the bay leaf, celery and thyme into a bundle and add to the pan, then bring to the boil. Lower the heat to a steady boil. Cook the lentils for 30–45 minutes, until just tender.

2 Meanwhile, make the dressing. Mix the oil and mustard with 15ml/1 tbsp of the vinegar. Add the garlic and lemon rind, and whisk to mix. Season well with salt and pepper.

3 Drain the lentils and discard the herbs. Tip them into a bowl, add most of the dressing and toss. Set aside and stir occasionally.

4 Heat the oil in a pan and cook the onion for 5 minutes, until soft. Add the cumin and cook for 1 minute. Add the spinach, cover and cook for 2 minutes. Stir, then cook until wilted.

5 Stir the spinach into the lentils and leave the salad to cool to room temperature. Stir in the remaining dressing and chopped parsley. Adjust the seasoning, adding more vinegar if necessary. Spoon on to a serving platter, sprinkle some parsley sprigs over, and serve at room temperature with toasted French bread.

White Bean Salad with Roasted Red Pepper Dressing

The speckled herb and red pepper dressing adds a wonderful colour contrast to this salad, which is best served warm.

Serves 4
1 large red (bell) pepper, halved
   and seeded
30ml/2 tbsp olive oil

1 large garlic clove, crushed
25g/1oz/1 cup fresh oregano
   leaves or flat leaf parsley
10ml/2 tsp balsamic vinegar
400g/14oz/3 cups drained
   canned flageolet (small
   cannellini) beans, rinsed
200g/7oz/1½ cups drained
   canned cannellini beans, rinsed
salt and ground black pepper

1 Preheat the grill (broiler). Place the red pepper in a grill pan and cook under a medium heat until the skin is blistered and blackened all over. Place in a bowl and cover with crumpled kitchen paper. Set aside to cool slightly.

2 When the pepper is cool enough to handle, rub off the skin. Carefully pull away the core and seeds, saving any juices, then dice the flesh.

3 Heat the olive oil in a pan. Add the garlic and cook over a low heat, stirring constantly, for 1 minute, until softened. Remove the pan from the heat, then add the oregano or parsley. Stir in the diced red pepper and any reserved juices, then stir in the balsamic vinegar.

4 Put the beans in a large bowl and pour over the dressing. Season to taste with salt and pepper, then stir gently until thoroughly combined. Serve immediately.

> **Cook's Tip**
> *Cannellini beans are always a creamy white, but flageolet (small cannellini) beans may be green or white. The salad will look attractive either way.*

Gado Gado

The peanut sauce on this traditional Indonesian salad owes its flavour to galangal, an aromatic rhizome that resembles ginger.

Serves 4
250g/9oz white
   cabbage, shredded
4 carrots, cut into
   thin batons
4 celery sticks, cut into
   thin batons
225g/8oz/2 cups beansprouts
1/2 cucumber, cut into
   thin batons
deep-fried onions, salted peanuts
   and sliced chilli, to garnish

For the peanut sauce
15ml/1 tbsp vegetable oil
1 small onion, finely chopped
1 garlic clove, crushed
1 small piece galangal, grated
5ml/1 tsp ground cumin
1.5ml/ 1/4 tsp mild chilli powder
5ml/1 tsp tamarind paste or
   freshly squeezed lime juice
60ml/4 tbsp crunchy
   peanut butter
5ml/1 tsp soft light brown sugar

1 Steam the cabbage, carrots and celery for 3–4 minutes, until just tender. Cool. Spread out the beansprouts on a serving dish. Top with the cabbage, carrots, celery and cucumber.

2 Make the sauce. Heat the oil in a pan, add the onion and garlic and cook gently for 5 minutes, until soft. Stir in the galangal, cumin and chilli powder and cook for 1 minute more. Stir in the tamarind paste or lime juice, peanut butter and sugar.

3 Heat gently, stirring occasionally and adding a little hot water, if necessary, to make a coating sauce. Spoon a little of the sauce over the vegetables and garnish with deep-fried onions, peanuts and sliced chilli. Serve the rest of the sauce separately.

Variations
As long as the sauce remains the same, the vegetables can be altered at the whim of the cook and the season.

Couscous Salad

Couscous has become an extremely popular salad ingredient, and there are many variations on the classic theme. This salad comes from Morocco.

Serves 4
275g/10oz/1 2/3 cups couscous
550ml/18fl oz/2 1/2 cups boiling
   Vegetable Stock
16–20 pitted black olives, halved
2 small courgettes (zucchini), cut
   into thin batons

25g/1oz/ 1/4 cup flaked (sliced)
   almonds, toasted
60ml/4 tbsp olive oil
15ml/1 tbsp lemon juice
15ml/1 tbsp chopped fresh
   coriander (cilantro)
15ml/1 tbsp chopped
   fresh parsley
good pinch of ground cumin
good pinch of cayenne pepper
salt

1 Place the couscous in a bowl and pour over the boiling stock. Stir with a fork, then set aside for 10 minutes for the stock to be absorbed. Fluff up with a fork.

2 Add the olives, courgettes and almonds to the couscous and mix in gently.

3 Whisk the olive oil, lemon juice, coriander, parsley, cumin, cayenne and a pinch of salt in a jug (pitcher). Pour the dressing over the salad and toss to mix.

Cook's Tip
This salad benefits from being made several hours ahead, so that the flavours can blend.

Variations
• You can substitute 1/2 cucumber for the courgettes (zucchini) and pistachios for the almonds.
• For extra heat, add a pinch of chilli powder to the dressing.

Cottage Loaf

Always a good-looking loaf, this makes a good centrepiece for a casual lunch or supper.

Makes 1 large round loaf

oil, for greasing

675g/1½lb/6 cups unbleached strong white bread flour, plus extra for dusting
10ml/2 tsp salt
20g/¾oz fresh yeast
400ml/14fl oz/1⅔ cups lukewarm water

1 Lightly grease two baking sheets. Sift the flour and salt into a large bowl and make a well in the centre. Dissolve the yeast in 150ml/¼ pint/⅔ cup of the water. Add to the flour, with the remaining water, and mix to a firm dough.

2 Knead the dough on a lightly floured surface for 10 minutes. Place in a lightly oiled bowl, cover with lightly oiled clear film (plastic wrap) and leave in a warm place to rise for about 1 hour, or until doubled in bulk.

3 Knock back (punch down) the dough on a lightly floured surface. Knead for 2–3 minutes, then divide the dough into two-thirds and one-third; shape each to a ball.

4 Place the balls of dough on the prepared baking sheets. Cover with inverted bowls and leave in a warm place to rise, for about 30 minutes.

5 Gently flatten the top of the larger ball of dough and cut a cross in the centre, 5cm/2in across. Brush with a little water and place the smaller ball on top. Make small cuts around each ball.

6 Carefully press a hole through both balls, using the thumb and first two fingers of one hand. Cover with lightly oiled clear film and leave to rest in a warm place for about 10 minutes.

7 Heat the oven to 220°C/425°F/Gas 7 and place the baking sheet on the lower shelf. The loaf will finish expanding as the oven heats up. Bake for 35–40 minutes, or until golden brown and sounding hollow when tapped. Cool on a wire rack.

Brown Bread

This seeded loaf looks rustic and is great for picnics and other *al fresco* meals.

Makes 4 rounds

20g/¾oz fresh yeast
300ml/½ pint/1¼ cups lukewarm milk
5ml/1 tsp caster (superfine) sugar
225g/8oz/2 cups wholemeal (whole-wheat) bread flour

225g/8oz/2 cups unbleached strong white bread flour, plus extra for dusting
5ml/1 tsp salt
50g/2oz/¼ cup chilled butter, diced
1 egg, lightly beaten
oil, for greasing
30ml/2 tbsp mixed seeds

1 Mash the yeast with a little of the milk and the sugar until it dissolves to make a paste. Sift both types of flour and the salt into a large warmed mixing bowl. Rub in the butter until the mixture resembles breadcrumbs.

2 Add the yeast mixture, remaining milk and egg and mix into a fairly soft dough. Knead on a floured surface for 15 minutes. Place in a lightly oiled bowl, cover with lightly oiled clear film (plastic wrap) and leave to rise in a warm place for at least 1 hour, until doubled in bulk.

3 Knock back (punch down) the dough and knead it for 10 minutes. Divide the dough into four pieces and shape them into flattish rounds. Place them on a floured baking sheet and leave to rise for about 15 minutes more.

4 Preheat the oven to 200°C/400°F/Gas 6. Sprinkle the loaves with the mixed seeds. Bake for about 20 minutes, until golden and firm. Cool on wire racks.

Cook's Tip

15g/½oz fresh yeast is the equivalent of 15ml/1 tbsp dried. It must always be crumbled into a bowl and then mashed with a little lukewarm liquid before adding to the dry ingredients.

Granary Cob

Serve this delicious Granary cob warm, so the house is infused with its welcoming fresh-baked aroma.

Makes I round loaf
450g/Ilb/4 cups Granary (whole-wheat) or malthouse flour, plus extra for dusting
10ml/2 tsp salt
15g/½oz fresh yeast
300ml/½ pint/1¼ cups lukewarm water or milk and water mixed
oil, for greasing

For the topping
30ml/2 tbsp water
2.5ml/½ tsp salt
wheat flakes or cracked wheat, to sprinkle

1 Lightly flour a baking sheet. Sift the flour and salt into a large bowl. Place in a very low oven for 5 minutes to warm.

2 Crumble the yeast into a small bowl and add a little of the water or milk mixture. Mash with a fork, then blend in the remaining liquid. Add the yeast mixture to the flour and mix to form a dough.

3 Knead on a floured surface for about 10 minutes. Place in a lightly oiled bowl, cover with oiled clear film (plastic wrap) and leave in a warm place for 1¼ hours, or until doubled in bulk.

4 Knock back (punch down) the dough, knead it for about 2–3 minutes, then roll it into a ball. Flatten it slightly so that it resembles a plump round cushion (pillow) in appearance. Place on the prepared baking sheet, cover with an inverted bowl and leave in a warm place to rise for 30–45 minutes.

5 Preheat the oven to 230°C/450°F/Gas 8. Mix the water and salt for the topping and brush over the bread. Sprinkle with wheat flakes or cracked wheat.

6 Bake for 15 minutes, then reduce the oven temperature to 200°C/400°F/Gas 6 and bake for 20 minutes more, or until the loaf is firm to the touch and sounds hollow when tapped on the base. Cool on a wire rack.

Irish Soda Bread

Traditional Irish soda bread can be prepared in minutes and is excellent served warm, with plenty of butter. You can use all plain white flour, if preferred, to create a bread with a finer texture.

Makes I round loaf
oil, for greasing
225g/8oz/2 cups unbleached plain (all-purpose) flour
225g/8oz/2 cups wholemeal (whole-wheat) flour, plus extra for dusting
5ml/1 tsp salt
10ml/2 tsp bicarbonate of soda (baking soda)
10ml/2 tsp cream of tartar
40g/1½oz/3 tbsp butter
5ml/1 tsp caster (superfine) sugar
350–375ml/12–13fl oz/ 1½–1⅔ cups buttermilk

1 Preheat the oven to 190°C/375°F/Gas 5. Lightly grease a baking sheet and set aside. Sift both types of flour and the salt into a large bowl.

2 Add the bicarbonate of soda and cream of tartar, then rub in the butter. Stir in the sugar.

3 Pour in sufficient buttermilk to mix to a soft dough. Do not over-mix or the bread will be heavy and tough. Shape into a round on a lightly floured surface.

4 Place on the prepared baking sheet and mark a cross using a sharp knife, cutting deep into the dough.

5 Dust lightly with wholemeal flour and bake the loaf for 35–45 minutes, or until well risen. The bread should sound hollow when tapped on the base. Cool slightly on a wire rack, but serve warm.

Variations
• Shape into two small loaves and bake for 25–30 minutes.
• Sour cream may be used instead of buttermilk, as both have a high lactic acid content and so react with the soda.

Onion Focaccia

This pizza-like flat bread is characterized by its soft dimpled surface, sometimes dredged with coarse sea salt, or as here, with onions.

Makes 2 loaves
675g/1½lb/6 cups strong white
   bread flour, plus extra
   for dusting
2.5ml/½ tsp salt
2.5ml/½ tsp caster
   (superfine) sugar

15ml/1 tbsp easy-blend (rapid-
   rise) dried yeast
60ml/4 tbsp extra virgin olive oil,
   plus extra for greasing
about 450ml/¾ pint/scant
   2 cups lukewarm water

To finish
2 red onions, thinly sliced
45ml/3 tbsp extra virgin olive oil
15ml/1 tbsp coarse salt

1 Sift the flour, salt and sugar into a large bowl. Stir in the yeast, oil and water and mix to a dough using a round-bladed knife. Add a little extra water if the dough is dry.

2 Knead on a lightly floured surface for about 10 minutes, then put the dough in a clean, lightly oiled bowl and cover with lightly oiled clear film (plastic wrap). Leave in a warm place for about 1 hour, until doubled in bulk.

3 Preheat the oven to 200°C/400°F/Gas 6. Place two 25cm/10in plain metal flan rings on baking sheets. Oil the insides of the rings and the baking sheets.

4 Halve the dough and roll each piece to a 25cm/10in round. Press into the flan rings, cover each with a dampened dishtowel and leave for 30 minutes to rise.

5 With your fingers, make dimples about 2.5cm/1in apart, in the dough. Cover and leave for 20 minutes more.

6 Sprinkle the surface of the loaves with the onions and drizzle over the oil. Sprinkle with the coarse salt, then a little cold water, to stop a crust from forming. Bake for about 25 minutes, sprinkling with water once during cooking. Cool on a wire rack.

Ciabatta

This irregular-shaped Italian bread is made with a very wet dough flavoured with olive oil; cooking produces a bread with holes and a wonderfully chewy crust.

Makes 3 loaves
For the biga starter
7g/¼oz fresh yeast
175–200ml/6–7fl oz/¾–scant
   1 cup lukewarm water
350g/12oz/3 cups unbleached
   plain (all-purpose) flour, plus
   extra for dusting

For the dough
oil, for greasing
15g/½oz fresh yeast
400ml/14fl oz/1⅔ cups
   lukewarm water
60ml/4 tbsp lukewarm milk
500g/1¼lb/5 cups unbleached
   strong white bread flour
10ml/2 tsp salt
45ml/3 tbsp extra virgin olive oil

1 Cream the yeast for the biga starter with a little of the water. Sift the flour into a large bowl. Gradually mix in the yeast mixture and add sufficient of the remaining water to form a firm dough.

2 Knead the dough for about 5 minutes, until smooth and elastic. Return it to the bowl, cover with lightly oiled clear film (plastic wrap) and leave in a warm place for 12–15 hours, or until the dough has risen and is starting to collapse.

3 Sprinkle three baking sheets with flour. Mix the yeast for the dough with a little of the water until creamy, then mix in the remaining water. Gradually add this yeast mixture to the biga and mix them together.

4 Mix in the milk, beating thoroughly with a wooden spoon. Using your hand, gradually beat in the flour, lifting the dough as you mix. Mixing the dough will take 15 minutes or more and form a very wet mix, impossible to knead on a work surface.

5 Beat in the salt and olive oil. Cover with lightly oiled clear film and leave to rise, in a warm place, for 1½–2 hours, or until doubled in bulk.

6 Using a spoon, carefully tip one-third of the dough at a time on to the prepared baking sheets, trying to avoid knocking back (punching down) the dough in the process.

7 Using floured hands, shape into rough rectangular loaf shapes, about 2.5cm/1in thick. Flatten slightly with splayed fingers. Sprinkle with flour and leave to rise in a warm place for 30 minutes.

8 Preheat the oven to 220°C/425°F/Gas 7. Bake the loaves for 25–30 minutes, or until golden brown. The loaves should sound hollow when tapped on the base. Cool on a wire rack.

Cook's Tip
Ciabatta is delicious served warm, but not hot.

Pitta Bread

Although you can buy pitta breads in any corner store, it is great fun to bake your own. They are delicious filled with ratatouille, roasted Mediterranean vegetables or salad. Make sure the oven is hot before you bake them or they will not puff up.

Makes 6

225g/8oz/2 cups unbleached strong white bread flour, plus extra for dusting
5ml/1 tsp salt
15g/ 1/2oz fresh yeast
140ml/scant 1/4 pint/scant 2/3 cup lukewarm water
15ml/3 tsp extra virgin olive oil

1 Sift the flour and salt into a bowl. Dissolve the yeast in the water, then stir in 10ml/2 tsp of the olive oil and pour into a large bowl. Gradually beat in the flour to form a soft dough.

2 Knead on a floured surface for 10 minutes, then return to the clean bowl, cover with lightly oiled clear film (plastic wrap) and leave in a warm place for about 1 hour, until doubled in bulk.

3 Knock back (punch down) the dough. On a lightly floured surface, divide it into six equal pieces and shape into balls. Cover with oiled clear film and leave to rest for 5 minutes. Roll out each ball of dough to an oval, about 5mm/ 1/4in thick and 15cm/6in long. Place on a floured dishtowel and cover with lightly oiled clear film. Leave to rise at room temperature for about 20–30 minutes.

4 Meanwhile, preheat the oven to 230°C/450°F/Gas 8. Place three large baking sheets in the oven to heat.

5 Place the breads on the baking sheets and bake for 4–6 minutes, or until puffed up. Transfer to a wire rack to cool slightly, then cover them with a dishtowel to keep them soft.

Variations
You can make smaller round pitta breads, about 10cm/4in in diameter, to serve as snack breads and for canapés.

Spiced Naan

Traditionally, Indian naan bread is baked in a fiercely hot tandoori oven, but you can use a combination of a hot oven and a grill.

Makes 6

450g/1lb/4 cups plain (all-purpose) flour, plus extra for dusting
5ml/1 tsp baking powder
2.5ml/ 1/2 tsp salt
7g/ 1/4oz sachet easy-blend (rapid-rise) dried yeast
5ml/1 tsp caster (superfine) sugar
5ml/1 tsp fennel seeds
10ml/2 tsp black onion seeds
5ml/1 tsp cumin seeds
150ml/ 1/4 pint/ 2/3 cup lukewarm milk
30ml/2 tbsp oil, plus extra for greasing and brushing
150ml/ 1/4 pint/ 2/3 cup natural (plain) yogurt
1 egg, beaten

1 Sift the flour, baking powder and salt into a large mixing bowl. Stir in the yeast, sugar and fennel, black onion and cumin seeds. Make a well in the centre. Pour in the milk, oil, yogurt and beaten egg. Beat well, gradually incorporating the surrounding flour to make a dough.

2 Knead the dough on a lightly floured surface for 10 minutes. Place in a lightly oiled bowl, cover with oiled clear film (plastic wrap) and leave to rise in a warm place for about 1 hour, until doubled in bulk.

3 Put a heavy baking sheet in the oven and preheat the oven to 240°C/475°F/Gas 9. Preheat the grill (broiler).

4 Knead the dough lightly again and divide it into six pieces. Cover five pieces with a clean dishtowel. Roll out the sixth to a tear-drop shape, brush lightly with oil and slap it on to the hot baking sheet. Repeat with the remaining five pieces of dough, keeping the unused pieces covered.

5 Bake the naan for 3 minutes, until puffed up, then place the baking sheet under the grill for about 30 seconds to brown the naan lightly. Serve hot or warm.

French Baguettes

Baguettes are difficult to reproduce at home as they require a very hot oven and steam to achieve the texture. However, by using less yeast and a triple fermentation, you can produce a bread that looks and tastes better than when mass-produced.

Makes 3 loaves
500g/1¼lb/5 cups unbleached strong white bread flour, plus extra for dusting
115g/4oz/1 cup fine French plain (all-purpose) flour
10ml/2 tsp salt
15g/½oz fresh yeast
550ml/18fl oz/2½ cups lukewarm water

1 Sift the flours and salt into a bowl. Stir the yeast into the water in another bowl. Gradually beat in half the flour mixture to form a batter. Cover with clear film (plastic wrap) and set aside for 3 hours, or until nearly trebled in size.

2 Beat in the remaining flour, a little at a time, with your hand. Knead on a lightly floured surface for 8–10 minutes to form a moist dough. Place in a lightly oiled bowl, cover with lightly oiled clear film and leave to rise, in a warm place for about 1 hour.

3 Knock back (punch down) the dough and divide it into three equal pieces. Shape each into a ball and then into a rectangle measuring 15 x 7.5cm/6 x 3in. Fold the bottom third of each up lengthways and the top third down and press down. Seal the edges. Repeat two or three more times.

4 Gently stretch each loaf lengthways to 35cm/14in long. Pleat a floured dishtowel on a baking sheet to make three moulds so that the loaves hold their shape. Cover with lightly oiled clear film and leave in a warm place for 45–60 minutes.

5 Preheat the oven to 230°C/450°F/Gas 8. Roll the loaves on to a baking sheet, spaced well apart. Slash the top of each loaf several times with long diagonal slits. Place at the top of the oven and bake for 20–25 minutes, or until golden. Cool on a wire rack.

Cheese & Onion Herb Sticks

These tasty breads are very good with soup or salads. Use an extra-strong cheese to give plenty of flavour.

Makes 2 sticks
15ml/1 tbsp sunflower oil, plus extra for greasing
1 red onion, chopped
450g/1lb/4 cups strong white bread flour, plus extra for dusting
5ml/1 tsp salt
5ml/1 tsp dry mustard powder
10ml/2 tsp easy-blend (rapid-rise) dried yeast
pinch of sugar
45ml/3 tbsp chopped mixed fresh herbs
75g/3oz/¾ cup grated Cheddar cheese
about 300ml/½ pint/1¼ cups lukewarm water

1 Heat the oil in a frying pan and cook the onion until well coloured. Lightly grease two baking sheets.

2 Sift the flour, salt and mustard into a mixing bowl. Add the dried yeast, sugar and herbs. Set aside 30ml/2 tbsp of the cheese. Stir the rest into the flour mixture and make a well in the centre. Add the lukewarm water, with the fried onions and oil, then gradually incorporate the flour and mix to a soft dough, adding extra water if necessary.

3 Knead the dough on a floured surface for about 10 minutes. Return the dough to the clean bowl, cover with lightly oiled clear film (plastic wrap) and set aside in a warm place to rise for about 1 hour, until doubled in bulk.

4 Briefly knead the dough on a floured surface, then divide it in half and roll each piece into a 30cm/12in long stick. Place each stick on a baking sheet and make diagonal cuts along the top.

5 Sprinkle the sticks with the reserved cheese. Cover and leave for 30 minutes, until well risen.

6 Preheat the oven to 220°C/425°F/Gas 7. Bake the sticks for 25 minutes, or until they sound hollow when they are tapped underneath. Cool on a wire rack.

Index

Veggie burgers, 60